THE PROMISE OF ALL AGES

By the same author

CHRIST AND BAHÁ'U'LLÁH
THE GLAD TIDINGS OF BAHÁ'U'LLÁH
(formerly *Wisdom of the East* series)
THE HEART OF THE GOSPEL
THE MISSION OF BAHÁ'U'LLÁH

THE PROMISE OF
ALL AGES

By

GEORGE TOWNSHEND, M.A. (Oxon.)

Sometime Canon of St. Patrick's Cathedral, Dublin
Archdeacon of Clonfert

*'It is my hope thy Church will
come under the heavenly Jerusalem.'*
'ABDU'L-BAHÁ

GEORGE RONALD
OXFORD

GEORGE RONALD, Publisher
46 High Street, Kidlington, Oxford
OX5 2DN

First published by Simpkin Marshall, Ltd., 1934
Reprinted by Lindsay Drummond Ltd., 1940
Second Revised Edition published by George Ronald 1948
Reprinted 1957
Talisman Edition 1961
This Revised Edition 1972

ISBN 0 85398 044 6

Printed in Great Britain by
Richard Clay (The Chaucer Press), Ltd.
Bungay, Suffolk

CONTENTS

EDITOR'S NOTE TO THE 1972 EDITION

Although *The Promise of All Ages*, originally published in 1934, is the first of George Townshend's writings on the Bahá'í Faith, today we see it as the second of an absorbing trilogy on the unfoldment of man's spiritual destiny, from the time of Adam to that of Bahá'u'lláh.

In *The Heart of the Gospel* (1939), Mr. Townshend explored this central theme and demonstrated from texts of both Old and New Testaments the unity of concept and purpose in the Judaic and Christian revelations, leading majestically and inevitably to the Day of God and the universal Kingdom which inspired their vision and their hope.

The Promise of All Ages carries forward with even greater clarity and intensity this theme of the oneness of world history. 'There is no world-religion extant which can be fully understood without a knowledge of its truth,' the author writes; 'no race nor nation nor tribe nor even individual who has not a designated place in the unfolding of the Grand Design of God.'

This perception of Divine Will as the central motivation of all human progress and achievement—Divine Will acting through a succession of High-Prophets to a culmination in world civilisation and universal peace—was the foundation of Mr. Townshend's life and work. His elucidation in this trilogy is a bequest to the thought and activity of our time which must win ever greater recognition, as will his exposition of the history and teachings of the Bahá'í Faith which this volume contains.

Christ and Bahá'u'lláh (1957) was the author's final affirmation, taking up the argument of his earlier books and extending and completing it with such masterly simplicity and force that his challenge rings out the world around, but above all to the Christians of the West.

This edition of *The Promise of All Ages* was revised by the author in 1948. His text stands as he left it, apart from minor corrections, but notes and bibliography have been added to assist the reader.

FOREWORD

This volume contains not only an argument but a story, a story of immediate interest and concern to everyone in the West; a story of men of vision and of action, the pioneers of a new era; a story of the first systematic effort to reconstruct the social order on a world-basis and to lift mankind to the level of a new social responsibility.

The central figure of this story is a Great Seer, who in prophetic tones forecast the character and magnitude of the Day of God then at its dawning, and by word and by example, in his Epistles to the Kings and in other writings, called on his own and other nations to reduce their armaments, to seek union and peace and to prepare for that long promised civilisation in which righteousness and justice should prevail throughout the earth.

Because he was ahead of his age he was misunderstood; and with all his followers was proscribed, anathematised, and cruelly persecuted. But a truth whose time has come cannot be suppressed by priests and tyrants. A strong fire smothered at the surface will be driven deep, will spread far and wide underground and will reappear later at a distance from its source. The spiritual ideals and noble peace-aims that now increasingly find utterance in western lands are as uprushes from a hidden fire, glimpses of that ordered and balanced scheme for world reform which was wrought out and promulgated by Bahá'u'lláh in prison some seventy years ago.*

The challenge of this story, of the enthusiasm of its heroes, their restless energy, their radiant faith, will bring

* Now over a century. (Ed.)

delight and uplift to every spiritual mind. For it is not the challenge of the cynic or the sceptic, but that of fellow-believers in God who with joy sacrificed all they had and all they were in an effort to establish World Peace on an imperishable foundation.

RIPLEY,
DUNDRUM,
Co. DUBLIN.

INTRODUCTION

This essay is an effort to sketch in the form of a continuous and coherent argument the religious teaching of Bahá'u'lláh on the subject of the unity of mankind and the establishment in this century of a universal and permanent peace.

Bahá'u'lláh set forth a comprehensive and definite scheme for a new world-economy. Men, he affirmed, would succeed in putting this into practice so soon as they sincerely realised the essential unity of the human race; but they could only attain this extension of consciousness through their religious instincts and their general obedience to one God under one name. He connected the idea of peace indissolubly with that of religion. Peace among the nations is only to be secured through men's common submission to a God of love. To build on any other foundation is to build on sand. Suiting the action to the word, he inaugurated a great religious revival, and such was his power that he aroused in those who turned to him for education latent energies of spirituality and love, so that with new eyes they saw the reality and authenticity of the ideals of brotherhood and concord and forgot their differences in their common servitude to the Most High. The revival embraced men of diverse nations and diverse confessions, uniting them with the ardour of a single purpose. It did not stop with its author's passing, but with slow and patient steps extended east and west. Today it has reached such dimensions that among those who accept his teaching his programme of world federation is beginning already to take shape.

The appearance, in such an age as this, and in a world broken into fragments by group-jealousies, of an earth-wide system of order based on spiritual faith is a phenomenon that should awake the warm interest of all religious minds. The presence in our midst of a movement on however small a scale which has taken peace as its first practical objective, and the whole world over is directing all its personal and educational efforts to this immediate end, is an asset which peace lovers can ill afford to ignore. Yet no Christian body seems to have paid any heed to the Bahá'í Fellowship or the teaching of its founder; and the public at large knows little or nothing of the world-wide peace work which he has inspired. In spite of glowing tributes paid by individuals of high distinction in Europe (scholars and scientists, men of letters and administrators, even by royalty itself) the Bahá'í movement remains little known in the West. Though it pursues with a fresh and youthful ardour the same broad ideals of world-wide righteousness and concord as are commended by the communions of Christendom, yet its appearance has been little noticed, and its potency little recognised; its reading of history has aroused no interest; its hopes have not been shared nor its warnings heeded; the spiritual splendour of the character of its founder has not been esteemed, nor the regenerative power of his teaching felt by any save a very few.

Some thirty-six years ago* when the movement was already well established in the East and had received not a little publicity in the West through the writings of Orientalists and travellers, its message of unity and peace was brought to our shores by one of its three great leaders and has since become the subject of an increasing literature in the English tongue. 'Abdu'l-Bahá, the son and the successor of the founder of the movement, was

* 1911–12. (Ed.)

hospitably entertained in London and travelled as far west as Bristol and as far north as Edinburgh. In public and in private, in church and temple, in mosque and hall, he presented the teaching of Bahá'u'lláh and secured at the time more than a little notice from the Press. Representatives of many callings and professions—clergymen, educators, journalists and others—met him and talked with him on the subject of his mission. A number of his conversations and his addresses were recorded and have since been published in book form. His hostess, Lady Blomfield, has recently contributed to *The Bahá'í World*, Vol. IV, an account of his visit to her home and of the throng of inquirers who for weeks beset her doors.*

Clergy of various denominations were among the callers. One of these, the Rev. R. J. Campbell, invited 'Abdu'l-Bahá to speak in the City Temple, and there 'Abdu'l-Bahá's first public announcement of the Message to a Western audience was made on September 10th, 1911. 'The Bahá'í Movement is very closely akin to, I think I might say identical with, the spiritual purpose of Christianity,' said the Pastor, in introducing the speaker of the evening. As if to endorse this statement 'Abdu'l-Bahá before he left the building wrote in the old Bible of the Temple:

This book is the Holy Book of God, of celestial Inspiration. It is the Bible of Salvation, the noble Gospel. It is the mystery of the Kingdom and its light. It is the Divine Bounty, the sign of the guidance of God—

and appended his signature.[1]

* See also Blomfield, *The Chosen Highway*, pp. 147–78. (Ed.)

On the following Sunday by the invitation of Archdeacon Wilberforce (Chaplain to the House of Commons and Select Preacher before the University of Oxford) 'Abdu'l-Bahá at the close of Evening Service addressed the congregation of St. John's Church, Westminster. As the published record of the meeting states:

> The Archdeacon had the Bishop's chair placed for his Guest on the Chancel steps, and standing beside him read the translation of Abdul Baha's address himself. The Congregation was profoundly moved, and following the Archdeacon's example knelt to receive the blessing of the Servant of God . . .[2]

On his visit to Oxford 'Abdu'l-Bahá was the guest of Professor and Mrs. Cheyne. Dr. Cheyne was (of course) a theologian of international repute, the chief editor of the *Encyclopaedia Biblica*, author of *Critica Biblica*, the *Prophecies of Isaiah*, the *Founders of Old Testament Criticism* and of other books; and he had a few years before resigned the Oriel Professorship of the Interpretation of Holy Scripture. On him the personality of 'Abdu'l-Bahá made immediately and permanently a deep impression. This meeting 'was fraught with pathos', wrote Lady Blomfield, who was present on the occasion. 'It seemed almost too intimate to describe, and our very hearts were touched, as we looked on, and realized something of the emotions of that day.'[3]

Three years later Dr. Cheyne expressed his mature conclusions as regards the Bahá'í movement and its three great figures (the Founder, Bahá'u'lláh; the Forerunner, the Báb; the Exemplar, 'Abdu'l-Bahá) in his *The Reconciliation of Races and Religions*.

'Abdu'l-Bahá reminded him of S. Francis of Assisi; but S. Francis 'despised human knowledge' and so

'Abdu'l-Bahá 'was a much more complete man . . .' 'No one,' he writes again, 'so far as my observation reaches, has lived the perfect life like Abdul Baha, and he tells us . . . he is but the reflexion of Baha-'ullah.'[4] Concerning the Herald or Forerunner of the movement, entitled the Gate or the Báb, the professor says:

His combination of mildness and power is so rare that we have to place him in a line with supernormal men . . . We learn that, at great points in his career, after he had been in an ecstasy, such radiance of might and majesty streamed from his countenance that none could bear to look upon the effulgence of his glory and beauty. Nor was it an uncommon occurrence for unbelievers involuntarily to bow down in lowly obeisance on beholding His Holiness . . .[5]

To Bahá'u'lláh, whom both the Báb and 'Abdu'l-Bahá honoured as the source and original of any virtue and wisdom that was manifest in them, Dr. Cheyne paid the highest tribute.

There was living quite lately [he wrote] a human being of such consummate excellence that many think it is both permissible and inevitable even to identify him mystically with the invisible Godhead.[6]

Adverting to the various avatars or incarnations which figure in many world-religions, he commented on the difficulty of obtaining contemporary or reliable evidence as to these, and proceeded:

The want of a surely attested life, or extract from a life, of a God-man will be more and more acutely felt. There is only one such life; it is that of Baha-'ullah.

Through Him, therefore, let us pray in this twentieth century amidst the manifold difficulties which beset our social and political reconstructions; let Him be the prince-angel who conveys our petitions to the Most High.[7]

Carrying his message to the Continent, 'Abdu'l-Bahá visited France, Germany and Austro-Hungary. At Budapest he was met by Arminius Vambéry, professor of Oriental languages in the University, whose books of travel and whose warm championship of British justice in the East had made his name widely and favourably known in England.

Vambéry wrote afterwards to 'Abdu'l-Bahá as follows:

... every person is forced by necessity to enlist himself on the side of Your Excellency and accept with joy the prospect of a fundamental basis for a universal religion of God being laid through your efforts.

I have seen the father of Your Excellency from afar. I have realised the self-sacrifice and noble courage of his son, and I am lost in admiration.

For the principles and aims of Your Excellency I express the utmost respect and devotion, and if God, the Most High, confers long life, I will be able to serve you under all conditions.[8]

America was included with Europe in the missionary tour of 'Abdu'l-Bahá, who thus spread the knowledge of the advent of Bahá'u'lláh far and wide through the Near and the Farther West.

His message, however, was not the first news of the movement that had reached the West. Tidings of the wonderful revival that had been started in Persia had been brought to Europe and to America by the reports of travellers fifty or sixty years before, and from that time onward references to it by Orientalists and others had become increasingly common. In his notes to *A Traveller's Narrative* issued in 1891 Professor Browne enumerates twenty-seven different European accounts of the Báb and Bábíism published in various centres—London, Leipzig, Berlin, Vienna, Paris, St. Petersburg and Pest. The most valuable of these he considers to be Count Gobineau's *Les Religions et les Philosophies dans l'Asie Centrale*,[9] more than half of the volume being devoted to the Bábí movement. Professor Browne writes:

> This most brilliant, most graphic, and most charming work is too well known to need any detailed description . . . not only are the facts thus obtained sifted with rare judgment and arranged with consummate skill, but the characters and scenes of this stirring drama are depicted in a manner so fresh, so vivid, and so lifelike that the work in question must ever remain a classic unsurpassed and indeed unapproached in the subject whereof it treats.[10]

Lord Curzon, whose work is not included in the Professor's list, dealt in his *Persia and the Persian Question* with the Bábí Revival at some length and in a tone of deep sympathy. Writing from inquiries made in the country in which it had originated and from which the government had taken such cruel measures to expel it, he spoke of the 'tales of magnificent heroism' which adorn its pages, of the 'pure and suffering life of the Bab, his ignominious death, the heroism and martyrdom of his followers . . .' 'Of no small account,' he says, 'must be the tenets of a creed that can awaken in its followers so rare and beautiful a spirit of self-sacrifice.'[11] He argues that since the new teaching in spite of persecution is spreading in Persia, and since its recruits are gained from among the nobler minds of Islám, the 'time may come when it will oust Muhammadanism from the field in Persia' and 'may ultimately prevail . . . '[12]

Professor Browne himself, however, did more to bring the Bábí Faith to the notice of the educated English public at the close of last century than any other writer. As Sir Thomas Adams's Professor of Arabic and Fellow of Pembroke College in the University of Cambridge he made himself an authority upon Persian literature and history and in his engaging style wrote much upon the subject. Among numerous works dealing with Persia his *Materials for the Study of the Bábí Religion*, the *New History of the Báb*, *A Traveller's Narrative*, *A Year Amongst the Persians*, not to mention briefer treatments, contain an immense amount of information on the early days of the movement. He had one experience in particular in the course of his investigations into the Bahá'í or Bábí cause which was shared by no other European writer and which gives to his account a unique interest and value. Neither he nor any of the authors aforementioned ever saw the Báb; but he, and he alone, met Bahá'u'lláh. In 1890, two years before the prophet's death, he visited Syria to complete his researches into the Bahá'í Faith, and it fell to his lot to become the guest of the Bahá'í settlement in 'Akká where Bahá'u'lláh was still held as a prisoner. During this brief sojourn he was granted an interview—in fact, four interviews—with Bahá'u'lláh and heard from the Teacher's own lips some of the outstanding points of his doctrine.

In his introduction to *A Traveller's Narrative* he tells how this experience came about, and proceeds:

So here at *Behjé* [sic] was I installed as a guest, in the

very midst of all that Bábíism accounts most noble and most holy; and here did I spend five most memorable days, during which I enjoyed unparalleled and un-hoped-for opportunities of holding intercourse with those who are the very fountain-heads of that mighty and wondrous spirit which works with invisible but ever-increasing force for the transformation and quickening of a people who slumber in a sleep like unto death. It was in truth a strange and moving experience, but one whereof I despair of conveying any save the feeblest impression. I might, indeed, strive to describe in greater detail the faces and forms which surrounded me, the conversations to which I was privileged to listen, the solemn melodious reading of the sacred books, the general sense of harmony and content which pervaded the place, and the fragrant shady gardens whither in the afternoon we sometimes repaired; but all this was as nought in comparison with the spiritual atmosphere with which I was encom-passed. Persian Muslims will tell you often that the Bábís bewitch or drug their guests so that these, impelled by a fascination which they cannot resist, become similarly affected with what the aforesaid Muslims regard as a strange and incomprehensible madness. Idle and absurd as this belief is, it yet rests on a basis of fact stronger than that which supports the greater part of what they allege concerning this people. The spirit which pervades the Bábís is such that it can hardly fail to affect most powerfully all subjected to its influence. It may appal or attract: it cannot be ignored or disregarded. Let those who have not seen disbelieve me if they will; but, should that spirit once reveal itself to them, they will experience an emotion which they are not likely to forget.[13]

His account of his meeting Bahá'u'lláh remains the only known record made by anyone from the Western world of such an interview. After some preliminary description he writes:

... a second or two elapsed ere, with a throb of wonder and awe, I became definitely conscious that the room was not untenanted. In the corner where the divan met the wall sat a wondrous and venerable figure, crowned with a felt head-dress of the kind called *táj* by dervishes (but of unusual height and make), round the base of which was wound a small white turban. The face of him on whom I gazed I can never forget, though I cannot describe it. Those piercing eyes seemed to read one's very soul; power and author-ity sat on that ample brow; while the deep lines on the forehead and face implied an age which the jet-black hair and beard flowing down in indistinguishable luxuriance almost to the waist seemed to belie. No need to ask in whose presence I stood, as I bowed my-self before one who is the object of a devotion and love which kings might envy and emperors sigh for in vain!

A mild dignified voice bade me be seated, and then continued:—'Praise be to God that thou hast attained! ... Thou hast come to see a prisoner and an exile ... We desire but the good of the world and the happiness of the nations; yet they deem us a stirrer up of strife and sedition worthy of bondage and banishment ... That all nations should become one in faith and all men as brothers; that the bonds of affection and unity between the sons of men should be strengthened; that diversity of religion should cease, and differences of race be annulled—what harm is there in this? ... Yet so it shall be; these fruitless strifes, these ruinous wars shall pass away, and the "Most Great Peace" shall come ...

Do not you in Europe need this also? Is not this that which Christ foretold? . . . Yet do we see your kings and rulers lavishing their treasures more freely on means for the destruction of the human race than on that which would conduce to the happiness of mankind . . . These strifes and this bloodshed and discord must cease, and all men be as one kindred and one family . . . Let not a man glory in this, that he loves his country; let him rather glory in this, that he loves his kind . . .'

Such, so far as I can recall them, were the words which, besides many others, I heard from Behá. Let those who read them consider well with themselves whether such doctrines merit death and bonds, and whether the world is more likely to gain or lose by their diffusion.[14]

Thus travellers and scholars had before the visit of 'Abdu'l-Bahá given to the Western public some account of the Great Revival that was arising in the East. Fragments of evidence remain to certify that these accounts, scanty as they were, made in some quarters a profound impression.

Professor Carpenter, Principal of Manchester College, stated in the course of a speech at Oxford on December 31st, 1912, that

The late Dr. Jowett once said to him that he had been so deeply impressed with the teachings and character of the Báb that he thought Bábíism, as the present movement was then known, might become the greatest religious movement since the birth of Christ.[15]

Dr. Caird, successor of Dr. Jowett as Master of Balliol, has been quoted in a similar sense.

Knowledge of the movement had spread beyond

academic circles. Leading magazines contained notices of it (the *Spectator* in April, 1892, for example; the *Scottish Review* in the same month; the *Academy* in March, 1895; the *Arena* in November, 1904). Inquirers from England and America too had gone out singly or in groups to 'Akká to gather from 'Abdu'l-Bahá himself further information.

Nor was the Bahá'í movement known on the western side of Europe only. Its fame had penetrated to Russia, and Tolstoi had given it his warmest approval.

He wrote in a letter, October 22nd, 1903, as follows:

> I have known about the Bábís for a long time, and have always been interested in their teachings. It seems to me that these teachings . . . have a great future for this very reason that these teachings, discarding all these distorting incrustations that cause division, aspire to unite into one common religion of all mankind.

> Therefore, the teachings of the Bábís, inasmuch as they have rejected the old Muḥammadan superstitions and have not established new superstitions which would divide them from other new superstitions . . . and inasmuch as they keep to the principal fundamental ideas of brotherhood, equality and love, have a great future before them . . .

> I therefore sympathize with Bábíism with all my heart inasmuch as it teaches people brotherhood and equality and sacrifice of material life for service to God.[16]

And again in 1908 in a letter to Frid ul Khan Wadelbekow:

> The teachings of the Bábís which come to us out of Islám have through Bahá'u'lláh's teachings been

gradually developed and now present us with the highest and purest form of religious teaching.[17]

The soil had thus been to some degree prepared for 'Abdu'l-Bahá before he came in person to sow through the West the seeds from which he affirmed a millennial peace in course of time would spring. His immediate achievement was to bring the movement to more general notice, to impress on it a more definite shape, to impart to it a fresh impulse and to direct the lines of its future course and progress. His influence as a teacher seems to have extended far beyond his audiences or the circle of his avowed followers. For some of the principles which Bahá'u'lláh had set forth in the sixties and seventies of the last century and which 'Abdu'l-Bahá transmitted in his missionary journeys have since then entered the Western mind and been accepted as distinguishing marks of what is best in the modern spirit.

Express tributes too to the beneficence of the ideals and the work of the Bahá'ís have been paid by many who are in no way affiliated to the fellowship—by Dr. J. Estlin Carpenter in his *Comparative Religion* (pp. 70–1); by Rev. J. Tyssul Davis in *A League of Religions* (London); by Charles Baudouin in *Contemporary Studies*; by H. C. Lukach in *The Fringe of the East*; by Sir Francis Young-husband speaking in *The Gleam* of Bahá'u'lláh's fore-runner:

Thus in only his thirtieth year . . . ended the heroic career of a true God-man. Of the sincerity of his con-viction that he was God-appointed, the manner of his death is the amplest possible proof. In the belief that he would thereby save others from the error of their present beliefs he willingly sacrificed his life. And of his power of attaching men to him the passionate devotion of hundreds and even thousands of men who gave their lives in his cause is convincing testimony . . . He himself was but 'a letter out of that most mighty book, a dewdrop from that limitless ocean'. The one to come would reveal all mysteries and all riddles. This was the humility of true insight. And it has had its effect. His movement *has* grown and expanded, and it has a great future before it.

During his six years of ministry, four of which were spent in captivity, he had permeated all Persia with his ideas. And since his death the movement has spread to Turkey, Egypt, India and even into Europe and America. His adherents are now numbered by millions.[18]

It is, however, in the invigoration and extension of the Bahá'í Fellowship that the effect of 'Abdu'l-Bahá's tour is most decisively marked. Groups of students were formed in England and various parts of the Continent as well as in America to study and promote the social and religious teachings of Bahá'u'lláh. Bahá'í books and magazines began to appear and multiply. The most useful text-book on the Bahá'í Faith produced up to the present time was written by a Scotsman—*Bahá'u'lláh and the New Era*, by Dr. Esslemont. But the most indefatigable worker in the Bahá'í cause on this side of the Atlantic was probably Professor Auguste Forel, whose enthusiastic propaganda made the name of Bahá'u'lláh more familiar in Switzerland than it seems to be in any other European country. He was a strongly independent thinker; but he explained that when after the war he came into touch with the Bahá'ís he found 'their principles agreed to such an extent with my scientific religion of the Social Good that I let the latter slide and became a Bahá'í.' In 1923 he founded the first Bahá'í group in Switzerland and devoted the latter years of his long life largely to the promulgation of the Bahá'í cause, testifying in his will to his hope for its future—'C'est la vraie religion du Bien social humain . . . *Je suis devenu Bahá'í.* Que cette religion vive et prospère pour le bien de l'humanité; c'est là mon voeu le plus ardent . . .'[19]

The extension of the Bahá'í Fellowship throughout the world at the present time, the domain of its special interests, the character and range of its activities, can be ascertained by a perusal of the ninth and latest volume of the biennial *Bahá'í World,** which is the official record of the progress of the Bahá'í movement, and from which (it may be mentioned) the quotations just made have for the most part been taken.

Here the Fellowship is shown to be established in more than eighty countries, the textbook *Bahá'u'lláh and the New Era* has already been published in thirty-seven languages and arrangements are being made for its appearance in several more.† In all these centres, and in all these languages, the one common purpose of reconciliation and peace throughout the world is pursued in accordance with the principles laid down by Bahá'u'lláh. Neither in this volume nor elsewhere in their work do the Bahá'ís enter the political field. The meetings of their groups are 'spiritual' assemblies; and their business is confined to spiritual and humanitarian matters. The primary concern of all is to spread the Bahá'í message of good will and peace and of the fulfilment of God's promise to pour out his spirit upon all flesh. Some years

---

* See vol. XIII for the years 1953–63; vol. XIV is expected in 1973. (Ed.)

† The Bahá'í Faith is now established in 333 independent countries, significant territories and islands; its literature has been translated and published in 501 languages. *Bahá'u'lláh and the New Era* is published in fifty-eight languages. (Ed., 1972.)

ago an English princess, the Dowager Queen of Rumania, published in Canada an encomium of the Cause, and said:

> . . . It is a wondrous Message that Bahá'u'lláh and his son 'Abdu'l-Bahá have given us. They have not set it up aggressively, knowing that the germ of eternal truth which lies at its core cannot but take root and spread . . . It is Christ's Message taken up anew, in the same words almost, but adapted to the thousand years and more difference that lies between the year one and today . . . If ever the name of Bahá'u'lláh or 'Abdu'l-Bahá comes to your attention, do not put their writings from you. Search out their Books, and let their glorious, peace-bringing, love-creating words and lessons sink into your hearts as they have into mine.[20]

And later came this renewed tribute from her Majesty to the beauty and the power of the Bahá'í books.

> The Bahá'í teaching brings peace and understanding.
> It is like a wide embrace gathering together all those who have long searched for words of hope.
> It accepts all great prophets gone before, it destroys no other creeds and leaves all doors open.
> Saddened by the continual strife amongst believers of many confessions and wearied of their intolerance towards each other, I discovered in the Bahá'í teaching the real spirit of Christ so often denied and misunderstood:
> Unity instead of strife, Hope instead of condemnation, Love instead of Hate, and a great reassurance for all men.[21]

Many lay members of Christian Churches (not the least earnest, not the least loyal, not the least grateful for the high tradition in which they had been nurtured) have been profoundly moved by 'Abdu'l-Bahá's presentation of Christian Truth. They have felt that here was one who spoke with a new conviction and compelling power, who truly loved Christ, and in the cause of his Heavenly Father had borne with rejoicing and exceeding gladness the bitterest persecution. His words, gentle and undogmatic as they were, had some strange power to pierce and germinate through which they sank into the heart and there bore fruit richly and continually. His exposition of the Gospels relieved for them old difficulties and met new doubts, giving back to them their trust in the Bible as the Word of God and in Christ as the Son of God which modern theology and the infection of belief had weakened. His description of what constituted the real Christian was the one which at the present time no organised body would unreservedly accept; yet they realised it might prove the only basis on which a lasting union of all Christian Churches could ever be effected.

> To be a real Christian [he said] is to be a servant in [Christ's] cause and kingdom, to go forth under his banner of peace and love toward all mankind, to be self-sacrificing and obedient, to become quickened by the breaths of the Holy Spirit, to be a mirror reflecting the radiance of the divinity of Christ, to be a fruitful tree in the garden of his planting, to refresh the world by the water of life of his teachings; in all things to be like him and filled with the spirit of his love.[22]

They felt that in him there was an authentic and radiant spiritual force which might prove the beginning of a general revival in Christendom of religious power, and that there was much in his teachings to aid and shape that restatement of the Christian Faith which is so greatly desired. They have wished that others more competent than themselves would give serious thought to 'Abdu'l-Bahá's expositions of the Gospels, and that the experience which had brought to them so definite a renewal of hope and of aspiration could be imparted to multitudes of their fellows. Nor was the sense of the urgency of the need of such a revival made any less by their despair of soul as they saw on every side the progressive decay of the old Christian loyalties, and watched in more lands than one, ancient churches subjected not to neglect alone but even to degradation or enslavement.

This essay, however, does not aim to put in order or to collect the teachings of 'Abdu'l-Bahá on the works of Christ. It seeks rather to promote in our time that cause which Christ so deeply loved and warmly blessed, and which has now become the most vital of all the causes in the world: the cause of peace, and more especially of reconciliation among the churches and nations of Christendom. It approaches this cause from a new angle and presents an argument which sets the whole problem of unity in a new relation to the movements of the hour.

The proposition which was the starting-point of 'Abdu'l-Bahá's message to the West and which filled the background of all his addresses was the announcement of Bahá'u'lláh that God had in this age fulfilled his ancient promise to mankind, and that by his intervention the hearts of men would be swiftly and completely changed, so that within this twentieth century universal peace would be attained and all nations would unite in founding a new world-civilisation. This theme has been taken as the subject of the present essay. It is worked out with special reference to our Christian religion, and is expressed in our Western idiom with sufficient clearness and candour (it is hoped) to represent faithfully the teaching of 'Abdu'l-Bahá.

What tidings to a travailing world could be happier than that the birth of the long-promised peace is at hand! Who will wonder that the Bahá'ís accepting this are the most hopeful, the most eager, the most active of all religious groups? If to others, amid the pettiness and arrogance of a self-infatuated age, these tidings seem in their vastness and awfulness strange and challenging; yet when one looks with saddening eyes and aching heart across Christendom and beyond its borders and sees everywhere the unwilled disruption of the social and economic order, the neglect of religion, the continuous enfeeblement of what is tender and noble and creative in human nature, and the unrelieved failure of all efforts to convert or to pacify those dark and desolating passions that threaten to sink all civilised mankind in final ruin, one wonders if any message less terrible than this of the blast of the trumpet of Israfil proclaiming the immediate consummation of the Apocalypse of God, would startle humanity from such a deathly sleep.

Perhaps this vision of mankind's essential unity may by divine grace not go unregarded, but may animate those who love God and his peace with a new sense of power, a new assurance of victory.

CHAPTER I

THE EPIC OF HUMANITY

Bahá'u'lláh revealed a sublime vision of human history as an epic written by the finger of God and proceeding along an ordered course to a climax, the nature of which was exactly defined before the story opened and the appearance of which at the date ordained by the Author no human misunderstanding nor opposition could prevent or postpone.

He taught that human history throughout its entire length was an intelligible and connected whole, centring round a single theme and developing a common purpose. From the beginning of the cycle to the present day and beyond the present to the cycle's distant end, one master-scheme is by set degrees disclosed. The stage upon which the action moves forward is the entire globe, with all its continents and all its seas; and there is no race nor nation nor tribe nor even individual who has not a designated place in the unfolding of the Grand Design of God.

This doctrine of the unity of world-history held in the revelation of Bahá'u'lláh a position of cardinal importance. He was far from being the first among the Messengers of God to reveal it. Those 'prophets which have been since the beginning of the world' and lesser seers as well as they have given glimpses of it to mankind, or have referred to it in symbol and in parable. It is indeed involved in all the historic faiths of the human race, and there is no world-religion extant which can be fully understood without a knowledge of its truth. But Bahá-'u'lláh was the first to lay on it so great an emphasis and to expound it at large and in plain terms. On it depends the significance of his own advent and the timeliness of his humanitarian reforms; and on it turns his teaching as to the aims and methods of Providence in its dealings with mankind.

This scheme is carried out by the power of God's will and it has its origin in his desire for the well-being of his creatures. Its aim is the training of the peoples of the world to live and to work together in harmony, and to establish by God's particular assistance a universal civilisation in which all the human faculties shall find at last adequate and complete expression. The attainment of this goal is in the Divine Author's eye the opening of the main movement of human history. All previous and earlier events are in the nature of an introduction. They are steps up a long ascent, causes of a desired result. However important they be, their meaning lies not wholly in themselves, but in the fact that they look and lead forward to a transcendent issue save for which they themselves would never have been called into existence.

Secular schools of thought cannot be said to have applied nor adopted any such broad conception of the integral unity of all human history. In past times, truths so large did not find easy entrance into the minds of men. So long as accurate knowledge of distant peoples was as hard to gain as accurate knowledge of past events, such doctrines would remain for scholars disembodied and unsubstantiated ideas. Today, histories of mankind on a comprehensive scale have become numerous; yet those of them which present the complete story as having an organic plot like a well-constructed epic are probably few indeed.

In the sphere of religion, however, the case is different. The idea that the course of human events is directed by a stronger will and a clearer eye than man's to a predetermined end is found in more revelations than one. It is said to have been mentioned by the founders of all the world-religions. Though it has not been in any past age of such critical interest as it is today and has not before been treated so fully as now by Bahá'u'lláh, yet it has never been kept wholly concealed from man. There are references to it in scripture or tradition which are clear enough to show that this truth is part of the common religious knowledge of mankind while slight enough to prove that it did not hold in any High Prophet's teaching the same importance as in that of Bahá'u'lláh.

The general fact that God ordains human events long ages before they take shape on this earth (somewhat as a dramatist will complete his play before it is embodied in action on the stage), was alluded to by Jesus when he said of the righteous in the Last Day, '. . . enter thou into the joy of thy lord . . . inherit the kingdom prepared for you . . .' (Matt. xxv. 21, 34); and again on many occasions by the Apostle Paul, as 'He chose us in him before the foundation of the world' (Eph. i. 4), and by Peter who speaks in a similar connection of 'the fore-knowledge of God the Father'. (1 Pet. i. 2.)

Muḥammad bore the same witness when he revealed that the first thing which God created was a pen and that he said to it, 'Write.' It said to him, 'What shall I write?' and God said, 'Write down the quantity of every separate thing to be created.' And it wrote all that was and all that will be to eternity.

More specifically, the Hindu religion ages long before there was a word for evolution, taught the God-guided progress of history towards a distant but certain culmination.

At some unknown date the Hebrew allegory of the creation of the world in seven days made a cryptic allusion to the procession of world-religions and to the final consummation of God's full purpose in the Seventh

Day, the day of maturity, completion and rest. The seers of the Hebrew people, lifted by inspiration into the eternal realm, would descry some sign or feature of the far-off Day of God, the fore-ordained climacteric of world-history, and in a mood of exaltation would give utterance to their predictive vision without fully comprehending what they saw or measuring the interval which separated them from its fulfilment. Isaiah cries:

> . . . it shall come to pass in the last days, *that* the mountain of the Lord's house shall be established in the top of the mountains . . . and all nations shall flow unto it . . . they shall beat their swords into plowshares, and their spears into pruning-hooks: nation shall not lift up sword against nation, neither shall they learn war any more. (Isaiah ii. 2, 4.)

Or Zechariah:

> . . . the day of the Lord cometh . . . And the Lord shall be King over all the earth: in that day shall there be one Lord, and his name one. (Zech. xiv. 1, 9.)

Or again Joel:

> . . . the day of the Lord cometh . . . there hath not been ever the like, neither shall be any more after it, *even* to the years of many generations . . . ye shall eat in plenty, and be satisfied, and praise the name of the Lord . . . that hath dealt wondrously with you . . . I will pour out my Spirit . . . and your sons and your daughters shall prophesy, your old men shall dream dreams, your young men shall see visions: And also upon the servants and upon the handmaids in those days will I pour out my Spirit. And I will show

B

wonders in the heavens and in the earth . . . The sun
shall be turned into darkness, and the moon into blood,
before the great and the terrible day of the Lord come.
And . . . whosoever shall call on the name of the Lord
shall be delivered . . . (Joel ii.)

Confucius, more than five centuries before Christ, outlined in his book, *Spring and Autumn Annals*, the ordained
Plan of History in brief but plain terms.

He divided history into three stages. In the first, which
he called the Stage of Disorder, the social mind was very
crude; there was a sharp distinction between one's own
country and other countries, and hence attention was paid
more to conditions at home than abroad. In the second
stage, the Advancement of Peace, there was a distinction
between civilised countries on the one side and those un-
civilised on the other; the range of civilisation extended
and friendship between nations became closer. The
smaller people could make their voices heard. In the
third and final stage, the Supreme Peace, there was no
distinction at all among the nations of the world. All
became civilised and met upon the level. Righteousness
prevailed and the world was unified.

Jesus spoke much of the Last Day (the Kingdom of
God as he usually called it) and of its near approach.
'The kingdom of heaven is at hand.' He did not stress, as
Confucius had done, the historical aspect of the coming
climacteric, but taking up the warnings of the Hebrew
prophets he spoke of the unexpectedness of its advent
and of the terrible jeopardy into which it would bring
mankind. Even in an age so late in history as this, a full
account of the development and destiny of the race would
have been premature. He kept the fullness of this truth
among those things which he had to say to his disciples,
but which at that stage they could not yet bear.

But now a new occasion has arisen. New opportunities, new problems, new perils, confront mankind; and with these new conditions has come the need of a new knowledge. He who, before the human race began, fixed the date at which that yet uncreated race would reach the apex of its course and attain the maturity of its powers, has now declared that the Date has come. He who, in dim and distant ages long past by, solemnly ratified with his people a Covenant and made to them a faithful promise that he would bring them all to his Kingdom in his own good time, has now in this epoch kept his ancient promise and fulfilled the Covenant in its completeness.

This present time is God's Good time. This present time is the Era of which since the beginning of the world prophets have chanted and seers have sung. Suddenly—unexpectedly—unawares—without observation (exactly as Jesus said) the fullness of the Glory of God has irradiated the globe from the east to the farthest west. The Day of the Lord has dawned. Keeping his pledge, God has thrown open to men a new domain of life and activity, has conferred on them new powers, laid on them new responsibilities; and he demands that they enter as quickly as may be into this new order of existence and fit themselves to these higher conditions.

The nature of those charges which in the Day of God are to be laid upon mankind can be gathered from a sympathetic reading of the prophets of Israel. Those seers wrote—as a great poet might write—with their minds turned towards God and their hearts lighted and warmed by ardent faith. They could not control the vision that was vouchsafed them: they could not complete it nor set it in its own environment and perspective, nor plumb its meanings nor yet count the years which should elapse before it descended from the realm in which they saw it to the realm of actuality. When the prophets are read in this spirit as Jesus and the evangelists read them, there rises into view a clear and boldly sketched outline of those world-developments which from the creation have been laid up to await the present hour.

The picture is one which has puzzled, fascinated and awed the Christian mind. The impression made by the vision upon the seer-prophets was profound. They write or chant in a strain of exaltation which finds its answer across the years in the rapturous faith of the Apocalypse and the controlled but not less deep emotion of the Christ telling of his second Advent. The strange scenes and deeds and wonders that appear in the picture are hardly more startling than the violent contrast of the colours in which they are painted. Here Hell seems to reach out to the gates of Paradise; delusion and enlightenment, despair and victory, the unlighted Pit and the sunshine of God's own presence seem all to have a place here, and through some purgation of Phlegethontic misery man hardly comes alive to inherit the promise of all ages.

The Event which the Hebrew prophets foresaw was not to be an isolated occurrence; it was one of a series of events; it was the Last Day of many days. But it so transcended all before it as to be outstanding and paramount. Its splendour outshone all previous splendours, and its blessings were so far above all previous experience and precedent that men would live in a new world and would not even remember the former things that had passed so utterly away. So full will be the Revelation vouchsafed by God in the Last Day, so glorious the effulgence of this supreme Theophany that darkness and error will not be able to withstand the impact of its might. They will flee and perish. The radiance will sweep across the entire globe from the east to the west. It will settle and abide in every land. Mankind will become one, and will be organised round a single central authority which it will recognise as divinely appointed. One law will run throughout the whole earth. National distinctions will not be obliterated; the various nations will meet upon a common level but will retain their separate identity. All peoples and races will share a common relation to one another. A Universal religion will unite the hearts of all. Mankind will form a single congregation, their God being recognised everywhere as one and the same God endowed with the same attributes and known by the same Name. The Glory of the Most High in its depth and in its height will be poured forth over the earth; and spiritual gifts, once the privilege of a gifted few, will be possessed by the many. War will be abandoned. The skill of those who made weapons of destruction will be turned to beneficent uses. All the world over, men will be able to enjoy their homes and their prosperity in security and peace.

(See, for instance, Isaiah ii. 2–4; xxix. 17–24; Zech. ix. 10; xiv. 9; viii. 20 ff.; Zeph. iii. 9; Micah iv. 1–5, etc.)

Such is the prophets' picture of the world conditions of the Last Day; such—believe the Bahá'ís—are the changes which man in this hour is called upon to make.

Prescient of the crisis and the difficulties that lay ahead, Bahá'u'lláh, eighty years* ago, with timely forethought, offered to mankind the knowledge that would enable them to shoulder the new responsibility about to be imposed upon them. He not only outlined a large plan of reform, but he explained, with an emphasis, a fullness and a precision not used before, the brotherhood of mankind and the unity of their development from the infancy of the race to the present time.

History, he taught, is in its length and breadth one and single. It is one in its structure. It is one in its movement.

* Now over a century ago. (Ed.)

From the beginning of time the whole human race has been subject to one law of development; and it has advanced age after age in accordance with one and the same principle and by the application of one and the same method. Its whole movement has one source and one cause, and is directed towards one goal. The unification of the world, instead of being an afterthought, or of needing an improvised miracle for its completion, is the normal conclusion of a process that has been going on since the race began. Each of the world-religions has its own set place within this vast economy. Each is radiated through a Master Prophet from God by one and the same principle and bears witness to some phase of one indivisible Truth. No religion has been exhaustive or final. Every one admits of development and invites it. If all were under God thus developed, each along the line of its own implicit truth, they would not move farther and farther apart, but on the contrary would approach one another till at last they merged and became one. The ultimate ideal of them all, while not the same as any one of those from which it grew, will yet be consistent with the essence of each of them. It is the universal religion: the fruit and the perfection of all that preceded it. He who accepts it on its appearance will not deny the ancient Faith of his forefathers; he will reassert it, and at the same time will accept all the other revealed faiths of mankind.

When all men know the certainty of their common history and their organic unity, then, said Bahá'u'lláh, on that knowledge will be built the temple of peace and the fabric of future civilisation.

CHAPTER II

THE SELF-MANIFESTATION OF GOD

Bahá'u'lláh not only filled in the fragmentary outline of universal history sketched by the master prophets of the past, but also revealed more fully the principles and methods through which God has ensured the continuous unfolding of his design. He would have men read history anew, seeing past events in a new perspective, grouping them in new relations and judging them by new values. The attitude which he would have them take in reviewing the story of mankind is the same as that which Jesus enjoins on a man in regarding his own individual career. The life of every man appears in the teaching of Jesus as in the last resort a drama of two wills: his own will and the will of God. The most critical of all matters for him is this inner relation between himself and his Maker. If it be wrong, all things will be wrong, and all his efforts will lead to nothing in the end. If it be harmonious, he will go forward under the guidance and protection of God, and his reward will be assured. Bahá'u'lláh would not have a man change his attitude in looking out upon the larger affairs of the world. Here, too, the central theme is the same. The vital concern for the race and for the nation, as for every man, is co-operation with the creative will and readiness to follow God's all-inclusive design for progress and attainment. Other considerations, however important, are for evermore less important than is this. He who would learn from Christ and from Bahá'u'lláh to read history aright, will assume this point of view as the starting-point of his thought and will see all events revolving, however remotely, round this unchanging centre of the Decree of God.

It may be that in classical literature illustrations of such a point of view are hard to find. Unfortunately, not many histories of note have been written on such a theme, and few authors have embodied in their works such a conception of the evolution of the human race. But there stands one ancient book of surpassing and imperishable renown which from first to last presents the course of human history as impelled by the might and the will of God as taking shape under the hand of those leaders of mankind whose sole aim it has been to execute his pleasure and to carry out his command. Whatever shortcomings critics have discovered in the Bible, and whatever the limitations of any of its writers, its general outlook upon mankind is that of the world seers and illuminators of the race, and it affords the most signal example now extant of that philosophy of history which is set forth by Bahá'u'lláh.

Bahá'u'lláh represented—in full agreement with the Christian Scriptures—that the unfolding of God's design is dependent not on the conscious good will of the multitudes but on the concerted efforts of a succession of Great Souls especially appointed and empowered for the task. These Great Souls, who are men and yet more than men, are the key figures of history: it is they who inspire the onward movement of mankind and determine the manifold phases of human progress and enlightenment.

For the development of civilisation does not proceed in a manner parallel to that which science discovers in the evolution of material life. Humanity does not advance in wisdom, virtue and happiness through the inward urge of some anonymous force or the uplift of some original inborn power of its own. Far otherwise. For all that raises him above the level of a human animal man depends upon a new and special principle that is not found on the lower stages of being. This principle is a part of the creative process, and is the cause of all that is noble and gracious in life. It is active today as it has been active since the time of Adam, and men depend on it now for their well-being as completely as they have done throughout the past.

This is the principle of God's Self-Manifestation in the human degree of existence.

The operation of this principle is the force that gives to history its direction and its continuity. The part that man's will plays in the perfecting of civilisation is a minor part. His dependence on the will of God is more complete than his ignorance realises and more abject than his pride inclines him to admit. Were it not for the special intervention of God in human affairs, so teaches Bahá'u'lláh, the earth would be the cockpit of base desires and raging appetites and man himself would appear as the most disagreeable and dangerous of the animals. History (if the annals of such a race could be called history) would have neither coherence nor meaning and the elevation of mankind would be impossible. Did not God show himself in this human realm, bringing down gifts from heaven, man would lack both the power and the will to develop. There would be no spirituality, no vision, no true life: the minds and the hearts of men would be wrapped in infernal darkness. For God not only leads mankind onward by his grace to a predetermined goal but in addition empowers them to follow his lead.

This divine aid is not given by the Most High direct. It is mediated through Great Souls whom God prepares, enduing them with his dominion and imparting to them the fullness of his perfections. These holy and transcendent Beings stand to humanity in the place of God. Through them alone does he bestow his blessings and his bounties on mankind, and through them alone can he be approached or known. To turn to them is to turn to God. To dishonour them is to dishonour God.

For God in his own being is for ever inaccessible and inscrutable.

To every discerning and illumined heart it is evident that God, the unknowable Essence, the divine Being, is immensely exalted beyond every human attribute, such as corporeal existence, ascent and descent, egress and regress. Far be it from His glory that human tongue should adequately recount His praise, or that human heart comprehend His fathomless mystery. He is and hath ever been veiled in the ancient eternity of His Essence, and will remain in His Reality everlastingly hidden from the sight of men. 'No vision taketh in Him, but He taketh in all vision; He is the Subtile, the All-Perceiving.' No tie of direct intercourse can possibly bind Him to His creatures. He standeth exalted beyond and above all separation and union, all proximity and remoteness. No sign can indicate His presence or His absence; inasmuch as by a word of His command all that are in heaven and on earth have come to exist, and by His wish, which is the Primal Will itself, all have stepped out of utter nothingness into the realm of being, the world of the visible.

... All the Prophets of God and their chosen Ones, all the divines, the sages, and the wise of every generation, unanimously recognize their inability to attain unto the comprehension of that Quintessence of all truth, and confess their incapacity to grasp Him, Who is the inmost Reality of all things.[1]

But since (so states Bahá'u'lláh) the purpose of existence is the appearance of the divine perfections, God therefore, that these might become known, sends forth certain Holy

Beings who are Places of Manifestation and in whom as in pure and brilliant mirrors the light and glory of the Most High are reflected in man's world.

> . . . the Source of infinite grace . . . hath caused those luminous Gems of Holiness to appear out of the realm of the spirit, in the noble form of the human temple, and be made manifest unto all men, that they may impart unto the world the mysteries of the unchangeable Being, and tell of the subtleties of His imperishable Essence. These sanctified Mirrors, these Day-springs of ancient glory are one and all the Exponents on earth of Him Who is the central Orb of the universe, its Essence and ultimate Purpose. From Him proceed their knowledge and power; from Him is derived their sovereignty. The beauty of their countenance is but a reflection of His image, and their revelation a sign of His deathless glory. They are the Treasuries of divine knowledge, and the Repositories of celestial wisdom. Through them is transmitted a grace that is infinite, and by them is revealed the light that can never fade. Even as He hath said: 'There is no distinction whatsoever between Thee and Them; except that they are Thy servants, and are created of Thee.'[2]

To the same effect spoke the Báb in heralding the Divine King whom God was to manifest:

> Verily He is the one who shall utter in all grades, 'Verily I am God. There is no God but Me, the Lord of all things, and all save Me is created by Me! Ye are to worship me.'[3]

And the Báb declared: 'Verily I am the first of those who worship him.' 'Abdu'l-Bahá, being asked to expound the degree of the power of the Manifestations of God, compared their influence over mankind to that of the sun upon the earth and the planets. Rendered somewhat crudely into English his answer was in part as follows:

> Consider the world of material things. The solar system is in deep darkness save for the radiance shed by the sun at its centre. All the planets of the system revolve around his might and are partakers of his bounty. He is the cause of life and light, and the means of the growth and development of all the beings of the solar system. Without his bounty no living being could exist: darkness and death would envelop all. In like manner, the Holy Manifestations of God are the centres of the light of Truth, the Fountain-heads of Mystery and of the bounties of Love. Their splendour irradiates the world of hearts and thoughts, and they shower eternal grace upon the world of spirits. They bestow spiritual life and their glory is that of the Light of Lights, the inmost Truth of Truth. The illumination of the world of thought comes from these Holy Originals of Radiance and Mystery. Without the knowledge and the instruction which they vouchsafe, man's intellectual and spiritual realm would be unbrightened, wrapped in utter darkness.[4]

The Bible testifies to the same truth, as when in Exodus iv. 16, God defines Moses' relation to Aaron, 'thou shalt be to him instead of God'; and again in John xiv. 6, etc., when Christ declares, 'I am the way, and the truth, and the life: no man cometh unto the Father, but by me . . . he that hath seen me hath seen the Father; . . . Believe me that I am in the Father, and the Father in me . . .'

These Holy Beings, standing between the Seen and the

Unseen and mediating between God and man, partake of the human and of the divine nature. As men possessed of physical bodies and rational human souls they come into existence at a point of time: there was a time when they were not. But in their true and inward essence, in virtue of that Fatherhood which as Christ said is in the Son and of their station as the Word of God, they are exalted far above men and belong to a different order of being. They outreach the human mind. Aspiration cannot soar to their dwelling-place. Whatever saintliness a man may acquire he can in no wise pass into the realm which is their home. No Isaiah nor Peter nor Paul nor Francis can ever share Christ's nearness to the Father.

As an expression of the Divine energy, these Vicars and Vicegerents of God have since time began come again and again to earth in answer to man's need, and they will in the future come again till 'the end that has no end'. The bounties of God are poured forth upon humanity ever-lastingly, and these bounties are bestowed only through the agency of these Holy Messengers. It is their function to 'breathe the Holy Spirit into the dead body of the world', to bring men from sleep to wakefulness, from darkness to light; from a merely animal life (which they count as death) to spiritual life. They impart virtue; and whatever virtues men at any time possess are not original but derivative, being bestowed by the grace of God's High-Prophets. The higher evolution of mankind is due to the influence of these Divine Spokesmen who lead the world onward, unfold God's redemptive plan by set degrees and give to universal history its structure and its unity.

Though mankind hitherto has regarded these High-Prophets only in their distinction and difference, yet in their most important and eternal aspect they are one and indivisible.

. . . they are all but one person, one soul, one spirit, one being, one revelation . . . they all abide on the throne of Divine Revelation, and are established upon the seat of Divine Concealment . . . Were any of the all-embracing Manifestations of God to declare: 'I am God,' He, verily, speaketh the truth . . .[5]

Bahá'u'lláh declares also that Jesus, '. . . addressing one day His disciples, referred unto His passing, and, kindling in their hearts the fire of bereavement, said unto them: "I go away and come again unto you." And in another place He said: "I go and another will come Who will tell you all that I have not told you, and will fulfil all that I have said." Both these sayings have but one meaning . . .'[6] 'Abdu'l-Bahá, writing for an English newspaper in 1911, stated:

All the teaching of the prophets is one: one faith, one Divine light shining throughout the world. Now, under the banner of the oneness of humanity all people of all creeds should turn away from prejudice and become friends and believers in all the prophets.[7]

In one of his letters to an American believer he wrote:

. . . in this sense Christ is an expression of the divine reality, the simple essence and heavenly entity which hath no beginning or ending. It hath appearance, arising, manifestation and setting in each of the cycles.[8]

This contemporary teaching does but corroborate and expand the evidence of older Scriptures. Muḥammad testified to the same unity when he said:

No distinction do We make between any of His

Messengers! . . . I am all the Prophets . . . I am the first Adam, Noah, Moses, and Jesus . . . Our Cause is but one.[9]

So likewise did Jesus in his statement to the Jews (John viii. 56 and 58): 'Your father Abraham rejoiced to see my day; and he saw it, and was glad . . . Verily, verily, I say unto you, Before Abraham was, I am.'

The immediate followers of Jesus learned this truth from their Master and testified to it. The author of the Apocalypse called Jesus 'Alpha and Omega, the beginning and the ending . . . which is and which was, and which is to come' (Rev. i. 8). The author of the Hebrews states that Moses esteemed 'the reproach of Christ' (xi. 26) higher than the pleasures of Pharaoh's court. And Paul speaking of the desert wanderings of the Israelites twice mentions Christ, saying that the Rock which followed them was Christ and that they 'tempted Christ'. (1 Cor. x. 9.) From another land and a yet more distant age comes the same teaching in Sri Krishna's statement: 'Age after age I manifest myself for the establishment of religion' (Bhagavad-Gita, iv. 8);* and in the same passage the Gita declares that whenever religion wanes and irreligion prevails there will be an avatar or theophany (iv. 7).

On the other hand, the High-Prophets appear to mankind not as one and the same, but as many and different. Each of them has two stations: one of identity with all the others, the other of separation from them all. The essential unity which subsists between them all, pertains to the things of heaven; their severalness pertains to the things of earth.

* A later translation of this verse is: 'For the protection of the good, for the destruction of evil-doers, for the setting up of the law of righteousness I come into being age after age.'—From Zaehner, R. C., Mahābhārata (Bhagavadgītā), Oxford, 1969.

> . . . each Manifestation of God hath a distinct individuality, a definitely prescribed mission, a predestined Revelation, and specially designated limitations. Each one of them is known by a different name, is characterized by a special attribute . . .[10]

In this second character of differentiation, they manifest absolute servitude before God, utter destitution and complete self-effacement.[11] Among men they walk in the greatest lowliness and simplicity, choosing a life of poverty, and even while they assert their Prophethood and declare the sublimity of their office, yet they behave personally as the meekest of the meek, the gentlest of the gentle. In the sphere of their distinction they appear in different periods and in different places and form a Prophetic succession or network, their influence spreading over all the world and all time. Each is like a physician prescribing a remedy for a particular disease (for the needs of mankind change and demand now one kind of treatment now another). Each is like a teacher, suiting the lesson to the capacity of the pupils. Each is like a guide, leading the wayfarers over a special portion of their journey. Each in turn founds a great religion; and though all religions are at heart the same, yet each has its distinction as in its purity the best possible medium for the spiritual energies of the people at the time. All the great systems of religion bear witness to the one Self-Manifesting God; if they set forth varying aspects of the Truth and if some are more rich and full than others, this is because each High-Prophet has his individual mission and suits his teaching to the requirements of the people of his age. If Moses gave a less exalted Revelation than Jesus; if he did not bid his followers return good for evil, blessing for cursing, nor promise eternal life to the faithful, the reason lies not in the limits of his own knowledge—God forbid—

but in the cruder condition of the world that he addressed. If, as 'Abdu'l-Bahá has said, the teaching of Confucius was less sublime than that of Buddha, the cause is to be sought not in the Vicegerents themselves but in the varying receptivity of the people to whom they were sent.

The material culture, too, which arises in every dispensation owes its origin to the influence and will of the High-Prophet. It bears a definite relation to his spiritual teaching; its character is determined by his decree and its limits are set by his command. All the world over, mankind has honoured the spokesmen of God, and has adopted their teachings. It reveres Christ, Buddha, Zoroaster, Krishna and other High-Prophets as its greatest leaders. But it has not looked on them as related to one another. It has thought of them as rivals, competing for the homage of the world. It has imagined that to accept the revelation of one is to deny the revelation of every other and that the votaries of any one High-Prophet are not loyal to their Lord unless they esteem him the sole authentic revealer come from God. It has balanced the High-Prophets against one another as it were in scales, so that when one goes up, the others must go down; and the zealots of one faith have despised all others as infidels and miscreants, outcasts in this world and doomed to perdition in the next. Thus the influence of religion, which ought to have tended to unify the peoples of the world, has through a misunderstanding engendered hostility and strife. The High-Prophets never spoke ill of one another: the antagonism originated with their followers. Krishna in the Gita does not suggest any criticism of any other avatar than his own. Jesus did not belittle Moses; nor Muḥammad, Jesus. Every High-Prophet claimed that his teaching was to be accepted as divine by those to whom he was sent and that it contained all things necessary to their salvation. None affirmed that his revelation was final or exhaustive: and in relation to earlier Revelators of his own succession he claims no more than that it developed the former teaching.

Now, in the Last Day, Bahá'u'lláh has dwelt at length upon the nature of his Vicegerency and Prophethood, clarifying, expanding and adding to former teachings on the subject.

With a new precision he reiterated all that had been revealed on this central and all-important mystery and emphasised in particular the interconnection of the Divine Prophets and their common service of a single Cause. He showed them all to be somewhat as relays of guides leading the people of the world up the sides of a mountain by separate paths to meet together at the top. For in the end, at the Last Day, all the peoples of the world are gathered under the shadow of one universal theophany. Different regions of the globe have their own prophetic successions. No High-Prophet appears to arise save out of the East, and in the East there are several lines of succession, that which has its place in the Holy Land holding the central position. Different periods of time have their appropriate measure of Revelation. There is no exclusiveness nor partiality in God's dealing with the children of men, but there is method, order and system.

Bahá'u'lláh quotes Sura xv of the Qur'án, where it is written: 'There is not one thing but the storehouses thereof are in our hands; and we distribute it not save in a determinate measure.'[12] He himself states in *Seven Valleys*:

> Although the bounty of the Bountiful One is continual and free from interruption, yet for every time and age a certain portion is ordained; and these are bestowed on men according to a certain quantity and measure.[13]

More specifically, 'Abdu'l-Bahá, in answer to a question as to the meaning of the recurrence of cycles in the world of existence, included the following statement concerning the supreme Manifestation of the Last Day.

> Briefly, we say a universal cycle in the world of exis-
> tence signifies a long duration of time, and innumerable
> and incalculable periods and epochs. In such a cycle the
> Manifestations appear with splendour in the realm of
> the visible, until a great and universal Manifestation
> makes the world the centre of His radiance. His ap-
> pearance causes the world to attain to maturity, and the
> extension of His cycle is very great. Afterwards other
> Manifestations will arise under His shadow who, ac-
> cording to the needs of the time, will renew certain
> commandments relating to material questions and
> affairs, while remaining under His shadow.[14]

The history of mankind takes shape therefore in the writings of Bahá'u'lláh as an organic fabric, its parts co-ordinated and set in their due place in a complete design. History, however long, complex and tumultuous in appearance, is at its core one and single and at its heart is sacred. The driving force which impels the movement of history is not the will of the human race, much less the action of some blind chance: it is the conscious intelligent will of a pre-existing Lord. This volition reaches out through all events and occurrences, great and small, and its range is limitless. History cannot be read aright unless it is approached with a knowledge of the Centre around which it all revolves and of the Energy with which it is all informed. He who attempts to interpret the changes of the world without reference to their Source will not be able—least of all in a crisis such as the present—to analyse the situation correctly or to act on it with foresight. The complete scheme of things is known in its entirety to God alone. But every son of man can now through the revelation of Bahá'u'lláh appreciate its general structure and acknowledge that there is no way of attainment or progress or hope or deliverance save by submission before God and obedience to his declared command.

CHAPTER III

THE SUCCESSION OF THE HIGH-PROPHETS

As Bahá'u'lláh has revealed that the High-Prophets are the dominating figures of universal history, so he has revealed that their appointed missions show forth the maturing purpose of the Primal Will and mark the most critical stages of human progress and the most important divisions of historical time.

The advent of a Divine Messenger does not seem to be represented in the canon or the sacred writings of any world-religion, and is surely not represented in the Christian Scripture, as an isolated phenomenon, simply an angelic adventure; nor is the Messenger shown as a solitary figure. He comes expressly as one of a line of teachers and is sent on a specific mission. He appears invariably in fulfilment of an ancient authoritative promise. Buddha foretold that in the fullness of time another Buddha named Metteyya should arise, and he taught that the Buddha's work was rather to revive religion and to re-create order than to bring into being something quite new.

As a man, brethren [he said, in words ascribed to him], wandering in the forest, in the mountain jungle, might see an ancient path, an ancient road, trodden by men of an earlier age; and following it might discover an ancient township, an ancient palace, the habitation of men of an earlier age, surrounded by park and grove and lotus-pool and walls, a delightful spot; and that man were to go back and announce to the king or his minister: Behold, sir, and learn what I have seen! And, having told him, he were to invite the king to rebuild that city, and that city were to become anon flourishing and populous and wealthy once more: Even so, brethren, have I seen an ancient Path, an ancient Road, trodden by Buddhas of a bygone age . . . the which having followed, I understand life, and its coming to be and its passing away. And thus understanding, I have declared the same to the fraternity and to the laity, so that the holy life flourishes and is spread abroad once more, well propagated among men.[1]

Confucius, too, is quoted to the same effect:

My work is to indicate rather than to originate.

Moses foretold a successor (Deut. xviii. 15). Speaking to the people of Israel he said:

The Lord thy God will raise up unto thee a Prophet from the midst of thee, of thy brethren, like unto me; unto him ye shall hearken . . .

The Hebrew prophets amplified this prediction; and attention was drawn to these utterances by Peter in Acts iii. 24:

. . . all the prophets from Samuel and those that follow after, as many as have spoken, have likewise foretold of these days.

John the Baptist quoted the words of Isaiah as indicating his own work and that of the Lord for whom he prepared the way:

. . . this is he that was spoken of by the prophet Esaias, saying The voice of one crying in the wilderness,

Prepare ye the way of the Lord, make his paths straight.
(Matt. iii. 3.)

As Moses linked his mission with that of his successor,
not less closely did Jesus connect his with that of Moses.
He made himself equal with Moses, claimed authority to
change the Mosaic law and represented his own work as
so much the same as the work of Moses that sincere acceptance of one would involve acceptance of the other:
'For had ye believed Moses, ye would have believed
me . . .' (John v. 46.)

Muḥammad 'recognized the truth of the signs, prophecies, and words of Jesus, and testified that they were
all of God'.[2] He declared indeed, 'I am Jesus.' He claimed
for himself the position of being the last of all the
High-Prophets that preceded the Supreme Theophany.
He closed the line—'I am the seal of the prophets,' he
said.

The two teachers, Shaykh Aḥmad-i-Aḥsá'í and Siyyid
Kázim-i-Rashtí, who heralded the Advent of the Báb and
the Dawning of 'The Last Day', bore witness to the continuity of the prophetic line. Aḥmad is represented by
Nabíl as conceiving his work to be 'to prepare the way for
Him who must needs be made manifest in the fullness of
time . . .'

He knew, and was destined by the Will of God to
demonstrate, that nothing short of a new and independent Revelation, as attested and foreshadowed by the
sacred Scriptures of Islám, could revive the fortunes
and restore the purity of that decadent Faith.[3]

Kázim, too, taught that the advent of the Báb and that
of Bahá'u'lláh were long before planned and announced
by God, being referred to, for instance, in the Qur'án:

And there was a blast on the trumpet, and all who are in the heavens and all who are in the earth expired, save those whom God permitted to live. Then was there sounded another blast, and, lo! arising, they gazed around them. And the earth shone with the light of her Lord, and the Book was set, and the Prophets were brought up, and the witnesses; and judgment was given between them with equity; and none was wronged.[4]

Which prediction Kázim (following Aḥmad) explained:

Verily I say, after the Qá'im [the Báb] the Qayyúm [Bahá'u'lláh] will be made manifest. For when the star of the Former has set, the sun of the beauty of Ḥusayn will rise and illuminate the whole world.[5]

Kázim used to speak, too, of the coming Advent as the times which the Prophets of old had longed to witness.

The Báb himself ratified this teaching of his forerunners, affirming that he was the successor and peer of Muḥammad who had borne witness to him, and that his particular mission was to herald the greatest of all Advents and the greatest of all Dispensations.

Verily I declare, none beside Me in this day, whether in the East or in the West, can claim to be the Gate that leads men to the knowledge of God. My proof is none other than that proof whereby the truth of the Prophet Muḥammad was established.[6]

And again, in the same gospel he is quoted:

I am, I am, I am, the promised One! I am the One whose name you have for a thousand years invoked, at whose mention you have risen, whose advent you have longed to witness, and the hour of whose Revelation

you have prayed God to hasten. Verily I say, it is incumbent upon the peoples of both the East and the
West to obey My word and to pledge allegiance to My
person.[7]

If an assertion of this truth even more plain, more full,
more emphatic be desired, it may be found in the words of
Bahá'u'lláh, for he has expressly based his work for mankind four-square upon the foundation of all the work of
all the High-Prophets of past ages.

Thus does every High-Prophet on his appearance draw
attention as part of his credentials, to his fulfilment of
authentic prediction; and before he departs, he foretells
the continuance of the prophetic line through his own
return. To this custom there appears to be no exception.
When Muḥammad said, 'I am the seal of the prophets,' he
did not mean that he closed the succession for ever and
that after him the gates of communication between God
and man would never again be opened. On the contrary,
he repeatedly said that he would come again.

Whether a High-Prophet in giving his accustomed prediction says: 'I will come again,' or 'Another like me will
come,' his meaning is the same, and his purpose is in both
cases to bear witness to the continuity of revelation. It is
not recorded in any prophetic line that the same individual
(the same mother's son) ever returned to earth to carry
on his own work, for though all the Spokesmen of God
have the same qualities, function and effect, yet they have
different personalities. The river is the same though the
water changes. If a man keeps a lamp burning in a room
its light at midnight will be the same as an hour earlier so
far as its qualities and its effects are concerned; but will be
different as regards the constitutional elements of light.
Nor will the case be altered if the light should be extinguished and again relit.

Jesus spoke of himself and his return in the first or the third person according as he looked at himself in one or other of two aspects. If he thought of himself as the Word of God, the image of the Father, he would say, 'I will come again.' If, on the other hand, he adverted to his human personality, he would say, 'When he is come,' because his successor would be a different human person.

This idea of the renewal of the same quality in another person appears in the Gospel with reference to Elijah and the Baptist. John in his spirit and his power truly was Elijah come again. But as a mortal being he was not Elijah: he was, on the contrary, the Son of Zacharias and Elizabeth and nobody else. Thus it could be said of him with equal truth but with a different meaning, that he was Elias, or that he was not; and between these two statements the contradiction is not real but apparent. When Jesus said that 'Elias had indeed come' he alluded to the spirit and power of John which was identical with that of Elias; and his pronouncement was not in conflict with John's emphatic denial—'Art thou Elias? And he saith, I am not. Art thou that prophet? And he answered, No.' (John i. 21.)

Whatever be his language, every Prophet, while asserting his Own Age, forecasts the unceasing systematic development of God's purpose through the future as through the past. It may be that in later times his followers do not appreciate this truth nor recognise what is involved in the prophetical succession. It may be they fall into exclusiveness, delude themselves with the thought that they have a monopoly of divine knowledge and that every other Teacher save their own is an adventurer. It may be they will hold these narrow views while they do not sincerely follow their own Prophet. But human errors, however well established, do not invalidate the truth. The common testimony of God's Messengers to their own place in history is incontrovertible; and one of the chief benefits of the existence in every Revelation of prediction is that it helps to impress upon the human mind the eternal co-ordination of advents and eras and the constant providence of an omniscient and all-powerful Mind.

The great world-task of Universal redemption is the common responsibility of all the High-Prophets. Each has his share, each his designated portion. Each takes the work from the hand of his predecessor and carries it forward till at the appointed hour he resigns his completed work to his own successors.

The powers with which these Teachers are endowed are transcendent and immeasurable.

> . . . in whatever age and cycle they are sent down from their invisible habitations of ancient glory unto this world, to educate the souls of men and endue with grace all created things, [they] are invariably endowed with an all-compelling power, and invested with invincible sovereignty. For these hidden Gems, these concealed and invisible Treasures, in themselves manifest and vindicate the reality of these holy words: 'Verily God doeth whatsoever He willeth, and ordaineth whatsoever He pleaseth.' [8]

The splendour, however, of the High-Prophet is not at all that which strikes every eye and commands the immediate homage of the multitude. As a man, he is marked by his simplicity and gentleness and lack of personal ambition. Often he is born of lowly parents, is obscure and impecunious. He is always a man of little human learning. For the execution of his mission he does not seek any of the means that are used by conquerors, kings and aspirants to high office, such as family influence, wealth, the arts of ingratiation or armed force. Compared with the mighty ones of the camp, the forum and the court, he appears as the weakest of the weak. In the face of violence, he seems to be defenceless. Subject like any other man to the ills that flesh is heir to, as hunger, thirst, weariness, sickness and the like, he lies open to his enemies and falls an easy victim to those who heap indignities and suffering upon him.

Yet, writes Bahá'u'lláh of the Prophets in the Book just quoted,

> . . . though their dwelling be in the dust, yet their true habitation is the seat of glory in the realms above. Though bereft of all earthly possessions, yet they soar in the realms of immeasurable riches. And whilst sore tried in the grip of the enemy, they are seated on the right hand of power and celestial dominion. Amidst the darkness of their abasement there shineth upon them the light of unfading glory, and upon their helplessness are showered the tokens of an invincible sovereignty.[9]

For the distinctive power of the High-Prophets is spiritual and intellectual. It is of a kind not possessed nor understood by other men. It operates on a plane of being beyond human perception. It acts directly upon the subliminal faculties of the race. It is creative; infuses into the deeper ranges of man's being a new power, a power of thought and of feeling that was not there before. It actually lifts mankind to a new level of consciousness. It quickens latent abilities and enables man to reach up a little higher than ever before into the spiritual realms which encompass him. The High-Prophet brings always a new Name of God—not only a new title but a new attribute of God: that is, he admits into the human consciousness a new attribute by which God is realised, a fuller conception of God.

His mastery of mankind is, therefore, such as no earthly potentate ever shared, approached, or so much as dreamed of. He is peerless, supreme, invincible. His sovereignty over mankind is described by Bahá'u'lláh as

> . . . the all-encompassing, all-pervading power which is inherently exercised by the Qá'im whether or not He appear to the world clothed in the majesty of earthly dominion. This is solely dependent upon the will and pleasure of the Qá'im Himself . . . That sovereignty is the spiritual ascendancy which He exerciseth to the fullest degree over all that is in heaven and on earth, and which in due time revealeth itself to the world in direct proportion to its capacity and spiritual receptiveness.

This transcendent spiritual sovereignty he explains 'resideth within, and revolveth around Them from eternity to eternity. It can never for a moment be divorced from Them. Its dominion hath encompassed all that is in heaven and on earth.'[10]

The development which the creative fiat of the High-Prophet produces in the hearts and souls of men appears in many forms. A new basis of agreement is realised among men, and people long sundered by prejudice of race or class find themselves united in strong bands of harmony and affection. The moral standard of whole nations is raised. New means of self-expression are demanded by society. New institutions arise, and gradually a new material civilisation takes shape better adapted than the old to the advancing consciousness of the people.

Reconstruction so great involves not a little demolition. The High-Prophet himself, though he endorses all the spiritual teachings of the last Revelation, does not hesitate to modify or repeal the material regulations and the ceremonies enjoined by his predecessors. These were suited to the minds of the people at a particular stage of their growth. But in a continuously changing world, rites and rules which are expedient today will not be so tomorrow. Outward modes of worship, and ordinances about feasts and fasts, about eating, drinking, marriage and the like, are not in themselves sacrosanct as are eternal truths. Such things, therefore, are regulated anew from time to time. But the Divine Messenger is never a revolutionary, nor is he always in the ordinary sense of the word a reformer. He changes the hearts of men and the economy of nations by quickening the process of growth rather than by external display of power; and the results of his influence do not appear immediately. He is studious not to let his cause seem to be political, and instructs his followers to observe a like carefulness. The thoughts and tendencies which he imparts to mankind are like seeds: they grow naturally by slow degrees. As in the vegetable world, trees that live long do not mature quickly, so do the great developments which the Prophet begins appear in their full significance only after long years. First, the people must be uplifted spiritually and morally; and when this education has been carried far enough, then progress in secular matters, in law, order, art, music, letters, and the like, next appears.

A High-Prophet founds the material civilisation of his Era upon a basis of spirituality and preserves it by the influence of religion. Centuries may pass before the new economy is established, but sooner or later appear it must. Throughout the whole of his Dispensation his dominion is complete and his will indefatigable. His precepts and ordinances are to be obeyed as from God; his teaching is sufficient for salvation: none can approach God save through him, since in him alone God is manifest and to turn from him is to turn from God. However unworthy the people of his help and however meagre their response to his appeal, his work cannot fail nor his mission go

unaccomplished. For God's foreknowledge covers all the
deeds of the people in every Age and the measure of their
disobedience is not forgotten in his predetermined plan.
Stage by stage, the divine purpose is advanced exactly as
foreordained in the beginning. Each Dispensation continues as a rule for many hundreds of years; but the length
varies very greatly. That of Abraham is said to have been
between five and six hundred years long; that of Moses
some fifteen hundred; that of Christ was six hundred and
twenty-two years old, and that of Muḥammad lasted
twelve hundred and sixty lunar years. The span of the
Báb's Era, however, was no more than nineteen years.
The precise date of the end of an Era is evidently fixed,
and is sometimes in an oracle designated by God before-
hand: the witness of scriptural prophecy shows this. But
the Divine Messenger during his lifetime seems not to
predict nor perhaps to know the year of 'the end of the
world' and of his return. Jesus prophetically sketched the
phenomena which would signalise his second advent, and
his description now is seen to have been wonderfully clear
and accurate; but he stated that its date was unknown to
any save the Father. '. . . of that day and *that* hour know-
eth no man, no, not the angels which are in heaven,
neither the Son, but the Father,' said Jesus. (Mark xiii.
32.) And on another occasion he spoke of the Father's
having put in his own power the times and the seasons.

But though the prophetic Dispensations are of various
length, the development of each Prophet's influence in the
world follows an unvarying course. It is not perhaps what
one would expect. It is not—like that of an earthly ruler—
subject to mundane chance and circumstance. Nor does it
climb to its *altitudo* at the end and so close in its greatest
splendour. It follows the same law of generation and
corruption, of growth and decay, which is observed elsewhere in the divine creation. Jesus likens the High-

Prophet's cause, which he calls in this case the Kingdom of Heaven, to a seed, the smallest of all seeds, which grows into a tree large enough to harbour the birds of the air. Ultimately the tree dies and falls. The cause of each Prophet springing from the minutest beginnings by slow degrees matures, striking its roots deep, and in its increasing strength spreading in all directions upwards and about; till when it has reached the limit of its power it slowly decays and at last, giving no longer shade nor fruit, it dies and falls. In another place Jesus adverts more specifically to the recurrence of growth and decay when he speaks of his Era as a 'generation', likening the ultimate declension of his cause to the sinking of human life into decrepitude and death: 'This generation shall not pass, till all these things be fulfilled.' (Matt. xxiv. 34.)

But the most common symbol under which in Scripture a Dispensation is described is that of a Day, the High-Prophet being its Sun, 'the Light of the World'. The splendour of the dawn which invests the earth with light and colour, and discloses objects to the sight of men, is a natural emblem of the animating and revealing effect of the advent of a High-Prophet; while the setting of the sun at the close of day corresponds to the end of an Era and the completion of a High-Prophet's mission.

Sometimes 'Abdu'l-Bahá would compare the coming of the Prophet to that of spring, likening his creative power upon the spirits of men to that of the springtide seen upon the vegetable world. For instance, in *Some Answered Questions* he writes:

Now consider the influence of the sun upon the earthly beings: what signs and results become evident and clear from its nearness and remoteness, from its rising or its setting. At one time, it is autumn; at another spring; or again, it is summer or winter. When the sun passes the line of the Equator, the life-giving spring will become manifest in splendour, and when it is in the summer solstice the fruits will attain to the acme of perfection, grains and plants will yield their produce, and earthly things will attain their most complete development and growth.

In like manner when the Holy Manifestation of God, who is the Sun of the world of His creation, shines upon the world of spirits, of thoughts, and of hearts, then the spiritual spring and new life appear, the power of the wonderful springtime becomes visible, and marvellous benefits are apparent. As you have observed, at the time of the appearance of each Manifestation of God, extraordinary progress has occurred in the world of minds, thoughts and spirits. For example, in this divine age see what development has been attained in the world of minds and thoughts, and it is now only the beginning of its dawn. Before long, you will see that new bounties and divine teachings will illuminate this dark world, and will transform these sad regions into the paradise of Eden.[11]

The year has its winter; day its night; and human life closes in a death. So each Era (following a spiral course) returns upon itself and passes back into the darkness out of which it arose. When the High-Prophet's Sovereignty has reached the Zenith of its Manifestation, when under his sceptre a great Church and a great civilisation have been established, when he is openly acclaimed the true Messenger of God, his least utterance held in reverential awe by the learned and the unlearned, when kings count themselves less than the simplest of his Apostles: then the Era passing its meridian begins a downward course. Enervation appears among the Prophet's followers; enthusiasm and obedience by slow degrees fail; faith

C

weakens, love grows cold. The old forms remain and receive still a superstitious respect, but men lose touch with the Spirit of the ascended Prophet, and the vast economy which had been built up under his protection lapses gradually into disintegration.

Were it not for this declension into the gloom of discord and unbelief, the re-arising of the Divine Light would not be necessary. Under an everlasting spiritual law it is man's need which draws down aid from heaven, and it is in the hour of spiritual death and misery that the Sun of Truth once more draws near and the dawn of a New Day breaks upon the darkness. Every advent, every avatar the world over has occurred in an emergency when the fires of religion had burned low and the people were immersed in base materialism. Jesus said it had been so in the times of Noë and that it would be so again in the times of the Báb and Bahá'u'lláh. So it was at the time of his own coming. In consequence, the Prophet does not meet with a general or ready response from those whom he has come to benefit. The people do not understand their need and do not recognise their deliverer. Self-complacent and absorbed in materialism of every sort, they are looking for anything except a new revelation of the Truth, a new spiritual birth, the advent of a new Lord in place of him whom they falsely profess to revere and follow. Not in one particular avatar only, but in one and all, 'the light shineth in darkness and the darkness comprehendeth it not'.

In his *Book of Certitude* Bahá'u'lláh sets forth the fact of this ever-recurrent blindness and explains its causes: his declared purpose being to help men to recognise the Theophany of this present hour.

Consider the past. How many, both high and low, have, at all times, yearningly awaited the advent of the

Manifestations of God in the sanctified persons of His chosen Ones. How often have they expected His coming, how frequently have they prayed that the breeze of divine mercy might blow, and the promised Beauty step forth from behind the veil of concealment, and be made manifest to all the world. And whensoever the portals of grace did open, and the clouds of divine bounty did rain upon mankind, and the light of the Unseen did shine above the horizon of celestial might, they all denied Him, and turned away from His face— the face of God Himself. Refer ye, to verify this truth, to that which hath been recorded in every sacred Book.[12]

He continues: '. . . throughout all ages and centuries the Manifestations of power and glory have been subjected to such heinous cruelties that no pen dare describe them'.[13] Bahá'u'lláh sets forth clearly the causes for this tragic and disastrous obtuseness. He states that they who wish to be able to identify a Messenger on his appearance 'must cleanse themselves of all that is earthly—their ears from idle talk, their minds from vain imaginings, their hearts from worldly affections, their eyes from that which perisheth.' Nor must they 'regard the words and deeds of mortal men as a standard for the true understanding and recognition of God and His Prophets.'[14]

Reflect [he writes], what could have been the motive for such deeds? What could have prompted such behaviour towards the Revealers of the beauty of the All-Glorious? Whatever in days gone by hath been the cause of the denial and opposition of those people hath now led to the perversity of the people of this age. To maintain that the testimony of Providence was incomplete, that it hath therefore been the cause of the denial

of the people, is but open blasphemy. How far from the
grace of the All-Bountiful and from His loving providence and tender mercies it is to single out a soul from
amongst all men for the guidance of His creatures, and,
on one hand, to withhold from Him the full measure of
His divine testimony, and, on the other, inflict severe
retribution on His people for having turned away from
His chosen One! Nay, the manifold bounties of the
Lord of all beings have, at all times, through the
Manifestations of His divine Essence, encompassed
the earth and all that dwell therein. Not for a moment
hath His grace been withheld, nor have the showers of
His loving-kindness ceased to rain upon mankind. Con-
sequently, such behaviour can be attributed to naught
save the petty-mindedness of such souls as tread the
valley of arrogance and pride, are lost in the wilds of
remoteness, walk in the ways of their idle fancy, and
follow the dictates of the leaders of their faith. Their
chief concern is mere opposition; their sole desire is to
ignore the truth. Unto every discerning observer it is
evident and manifest that had these people in the days
of each of the Manifestations of the Sun of Truth
sanctified their eyes, their ears, and their hearts from
whatever they had seen, heard, and felt, they surely
would not have been deprived of beholding the beauty
of God, nor strayed far from the habitations of glory.
But having weighed the testimony of God by the
standard of their own knowledge, gleaned from the
teachings of the leaders of their faith, and found it at
variance with their limited understanding, they arose
to perpetrate such unseemly acts.

Leaders of religion, in every age, have hindered their
people from attaining the shores of eternal salvation,
inasmuch as they held the reins of authority in their

mighty grasp. Some for the lust of leadership, others through want of knowledge and understanding, have been the cause of the deprivation of the people. By their sanction and authority, every Prophet of God hath drunk from the chalice of sacrifice, and winged His flight unto the heights of glory. What unspeakable cruelties they that have occupied the seats of authority and learning have inflicted upon the true Monarchs of the world, those Gems of divine virtue! Content with a transitory dominion, they have deprived themselves of an everlasting sovereignty. Thus, their eyes beheld not the light of the countenance of the Well-Beloved, nor did their ears hearken unto the sweet melodies of the Bird of Desire. For this reason, in all sacred books mention hath been made of the divines of every age . . .

. . . The denials and protestations of these leaders of religion have, in the main, been due to their lack of knowledge and understanding. Those words uttered by the Revealers of the beauty of the one true God, setting forth the signs . . . of the Manifestation to come, they never understood nor fathomed. Hence they raised the standard of revolt, and stirred up mischief and sedition.[15]

The mission of every Prophet must, therefore, at its birth and in its infancy face criticism from the sophists and persecution from the powerful. His Cause becomes the touchstone by which the Lord of Truth tests the souls of men for the purity of their faith and the reality of their devotion. It separates those who seemed to be bound by close ties: comrade from comrade, friend from friend, brother from brother, father from son.

Those whom the divine assay proves to be true believers are, if they arise to confess their faith and to propagate the Cause, endowed by the Prophet with a superhuman power.

Their witness to him cannot be gainsaid. Though they may be few or poor or unlearned or obscure, or afflicted with bodily infirmity; though they be hampered by opposition or silenced by imprisonment or martyrdom, yet the Message they transmit is caught by others, and passed on. At last it prevails. It is accepted on every side and acknowledged by all as the very Word of God. The period of transition, known in Scripture as the Day of Judgment, is then complete. The second period of the Era—that of material development—opens, and in due course, as in all previous Eras, the rolling centuries bring again the recurrent phenomena of weakness and decay.

Such is the procession of the Ages which the High-Prophets in their order, one by one, lead onward down the high road of historic time. All are in structure and in movement alike; and all are made after that same cyclic pattern to which in nature the day, the year and the life of man also conform. Yet each Age, while indisseverably bound to all the rest, is a complete unit, serving its own special purpose and having no duplicate in the entire series.

The progress of mankind as it appears in history is not even, constant, uniform. It resembles in its motion the incoming tide with waves that advance and recede, rather than a smooth-sliding stream. To use another figure. The High-Prophet is in relation to mankind as the heart is to the human body. The life which he infuses into the world has its rhythmic beats like the blood which pulses through the arteries. These flowing waves, these pulses of the heart, are impulses of the divine energy and constitute the vital events of history. The advents of the High-Prophets fix the great historical epochs, and the duration of their missions marks the great historical divisions of time.

CHAPTER IV

THE MISSION OF THE LORD CHRIST

The task of Christ differed from that of any of the High-Prophets who preceded him in that to him was assigned the duty of announcement that the Supreme Advent of all time was now at hand and of completing the education of mankind for that august event. His Dispensation stands apart from all before it in that it crowns the period of preparation and opens directly into that Age of God for which all previous Messengers had made ready the way.

Never till now was it given to men to view the work of Christ in its true perspective or to discern the full proportions of his wisdom and beneficence. Those who have felt themselves forgiven and redeemed through him have throughout the Christian Era chanted in many accents his praise; and all that their lips could utter would not tell the tale of their gratitude nor express the felicity which he had brought to their lives. Historians, in belief and in unbelief, have extolled the radiant beauty of his character, the elevating influence of his teachings, and the transformation of the Western world which has been effected through his power. But not until the Dawn of God broke over the earth, not until Bahá'u'lláh told of the progressive revelation of God through a world-old sequence of Divine Teachers, could men regard Christ's Message in its larger aspects or set it in its due relation to the complete redemptive purpose of the Eternal God.

Now that the faithful look back upon the past through the portals of God's Age of Gold, it is possible to discern from a new angle values in Christ's teaching that before were hidden and to probe with a clearer insight the bearing and significance of many of his utterances. The directions of Jesus were, of course, like those of every other High-Prophet, measured with loving care to the needs and capacities of the people to whom he ministered. Out of the limitless treasury of his knowledge he bestowed on them that which would help them most. But his special mission of preparing humanity for the great climacteric that drew so near gave to his teaching a special character. The substance of his revelation was designed to prepare mankind for that severe test of love and spirituality to which they were so soon to be subjected. His heart was fixed upon the Kingdom that was to be, and his central aim was to fit the people for this great enfranchisement and to strengthen them against the perils of the awful Day of Doom.

Now in the twentieth century when that Doomsday has come upon us, when the principles of that Kingdom have been divinely revealed and when its outline is taking visible shape throughout the earth, now for the first time the believer is enabled to discern how the Revelation of Christ was so conceived as to lead by a natural gradation into the Age of Bahá'u'lláh; now for the first time he can appreciate something of the foreknowledge and the wisdom of him whose far-reaching vision swept down the long vista of his own Dispensation to the happenings of this newborn Day of God.

The central message of Jesus was his promise and his warning that before long (at the end of one more Era, the Era then begun) God would in deed and in fact establish the Kingdom upon earth; its foundations would be laid in the hearts of men, and those who were found to be unworthy would be destroyed. The Event of which poets had dreamed, which seers had descried, which prophets had predicted, was soon to be no more a dream or a hope or a forecast but an accomplished fact of history.

This was from the first to the last throughout his ministry the great theme of Jesus' preaching, as it had been the theme of his forerunner, John:

From that time Jesus began to preach, and to say, Repent: for the kingdom of heaven is at hand. (Matt. iv. 17.)

The coming of that Kingdom was by this command to be the prayer of the faithful all through his Dispensation: 'Thy kingdom come, thy will be done on earth as in heaven.' And the prediction that one day he will again hold communion with the faithful on earth in his Father's Kingdom is one of the parting thoughts of his discourse at the Last Supper.

Jesus' revelation was not exclusively spiritual. It was in part historical. He opened not only the gates of a future life beyond the grave, but the gates of humanity's future life upon the earth. He teaches men not only to look inward where God has set his shrine in the human heart, but to look forward to a time when God shall set his tabernacle among men. Hope became a Christian virtue; and the object of hope was not only the spiritual salvation of the individual but the social salvation of the race. He bade believers have no fear, for it was the Father's pleasure, to give them the Kingdom (in which utterance, of course, as when he said, 'Watch, for ye know not what hour your Lord cometh,' or 'I am with you always even to the end of the dispensation,' he addressed not only those who stood before him at the moment but all the faithful of his 'generation', and after). The Gospel of Matthew quotes four of Christ's most famous discourses. In every one of these—the Sermon on the Mount, the charge to the Twelve, the Seven Parables of chapter xiii and the Words on Mount Olivet—reference is made to the coming of the Father's Kingdom; and in one of them, and not the least sublime, no leading reference is made to anything else.

The intensity of Jesus' spirituality, the vigour of his insistence that the vital matter in life is the right relation of the individual soul to God, seem to make more startling, more arresting by contrast, those historical predictions in which he deals with outward happenings and world-wide events and speaks not alone to the individual but especially to nations and the human race as a whole.

Not that in their character and essence the laws and injunctions of Jesus are different from his forecasts and promises. The outlook and the spirit is ever unchanging. Indeed, in the light of the further revelation of Bahá-'u'lláh, the connection between the two portions of Jesus' teaching is seen to be close and intimate. The distinction is real; yet it is now evident that the spiritual principles which Christ most strongly urged are the self-same principles on which his Father's Kingdom in the world today is based. His religious teachings seem to have been directed to the purpose of preparing mankind for the promised gift of the Kingdom, and to have been designed to elevate and strengthen them for the task of establishing it upon the earth.

For the Kingdom of the Father is indeed an earthly kingdom in the sense that it is set down four-square upon the solid earth for all men to see it, know it and inhabit it. But it is not less certainly a spiritual kingdom. The rule of the Father is primarily over the hearts of men, and it is as the winner of their hearts that he controls their wills and their actions. Till the human heart is opened to God and is made fit and ready to receive him, such a rule is impossible; and it is to the preparation of the heart for God that Christ addresses the main body of his teaching. Set the instruction of Jesus beside that of the mighty

Prophet who preceded him, and in nothing does it show a greater heightening than in its insistence on spirituality and love. Moses, meting his message to a cruder people in a cruder age, had said nothing of eternal life. His religion was a religion of one world. They who faithfully obeyed the commandments of God would dwell long in the land enjoying peace and plenty. But Christ's was a religion of two worlds, the outer and the inner, the material and the spiritual; and of the two by far the more important was the latter. He did not teach believers to set much store by temporal rewards, but rather to desire the everlasting blessedness of the vision of God, admission to his presence and the enjoyment of his mercy. Moses had given a comprehensive code of statutes and regulations; Jesus—so far as our canon informs us—gave two material ordinances only. He loosed men from the law of the sabbath and made more tight the law of divorce. He removed a complicated system of ritual and material sacrifice; and no record remains of his having instituted in its place more than two ceremonies, both of which were essentially symbolic. In contrast to the offerings demanded by the old law these rites involve no material outlay of any moment. The ancient ordinance that no worshipper should appear before the Lord empty-handed was not fulfilled in them. No gift of bullock, ram or sheep, not even of a little dove or two young pigeons, was called for. A running brook, an ordinary meal, supplied the Christian with all he needed for baptism and the breaking of bread. The meaning and the value of the observance lay wholly in that spiritual thing which is signified. The baptism with water typified that baptism with the Holy Spirit and the fire of the love of God (spoken of by John) which Christ conferred on those who were able to receive it. The blessedness of the memorial feast was its renewing of that spiritual love which gave to the Lord's last passover its unique and imperishable glory.

Moses, like every High-Prophet before or since, proclaimed the law of love. Every High-Prophet has done so—'All laws and ordinances,' said Bahá'u'lláh, 'have been changed according to the requirements of the times, except the law of love, which like a fountain ever flows and the course of which never suffers change.'[1] Moses commanded (Deut. vi. 5), '. . . thou shalt love the Lord thy God with all thine heart, and with all thy soul, and with all thy might' and (Lev. xix. 18), '. . . thou shalt love thy neighbour as thyself'. But Jesus revealed the law more fully and insisted on a larger obedience to it. 'A new commandment I give unto you, That ye love one another. . . ' He made love the test of discipleship. 'By this shall all *men* know that ye are my disciples, if ye have love one to another.' (John xiii. 34–5.) If he taught that God was Spirit, men learned from him that God was Love. The whole duty of man towards his Maker and towards his fellow-creature was comprehended in the practice of Love. When he carried men to the summit of all his most exalted and exacting demands, he bade them to be perfect as their Father, whose nature he revealed as being Spirit and Love.

Had men during the Christian Era learned from their Master this lesson of spirituality and love, the establishment of the Father's Kingdom upon earth would be an easy task today. The fact that the Kingdom has—as the Bahá'ís believe—in very fact been inaugurated, stands now fixed upon irremovable foundations, and takes shape amidst the chaos of the nations, is the greatest proof existing of the wisdom and the power and the triumph of the Lord Christ.

Not only did Christ reveal the leading principles of the Kingdom which was—he said—so soon to come, but he gave many signs by which the approach of that Kingdom and of his own advent might be recognised. The date he did not give: it was known only to the Father. But he presaged a number of events and omens, some of them unmistakable and portentous, for which he bade men watch. The period was to be distant. The Gospel would be carried to all lands; and, nevertheless, before the Son of Man came, faith would be hard to find and the people growing careless and disobedient, would indulge in oppression and tyranny and would give themselves up to worldly pursuits. The fate of the Jews, however, would be the most definite prognostic of the time of the end. During the Christian Era they were to be scattered abroad and held in exile. When they had served their sentence and were permitted to return to their own land, the world might know that an epoch had ended and a new world-age begun.

Such a prediction was so clear that it would seem Christ had made any failure to identify his coming impossible. Yet he went further. He spoke repeatedly about his own coming. His language was (as always) simple, yet it was such as to arrest attention and to demand scrutiny. He announced that he would come with power in the glory of the Father; that he would send his angels throughout the world and would destroy the ungodly; and that his splendour would shine in the darkness from the east to the west. But he also said with not less emphasis that his coming would take mankind by surprise: as a thief enters stealthily at night and is in the house while the master sleeps and knows it not, so he would come into a world wrapt in spiritual ignorance and would not be observed by those to whom he came.

It is not put on record that his disciples asked him the meaning of forewarnings so important and seemingly so contradictory, nor is there extant the explanation of any inconsistency. He gave men enough information to guide them aright when the emergency arose, and left the rest to their own efforts.

The tone in which he delivered these prophecies about the dawn of the Last Day was not that which his hearers might have expected. He did not speak of the approach of world-redemption in a joyous and triumphant strain. On the contrary, his words were those of premonition and anxiety. Though the great Day which he had the privilege to foretell was the time of the Victory of God, was to purge away sorrow and tears and spiritual death, and to usher in the reign of concord and peace and divine felicity when the righteous would shine forth as the sun in the Kingdom of the Father, yet his language about its drawing near was imbued with grave foreboding. He dwelt on the thought of a Great Assize in which he would figure as Judge and would be called on to condemn many who used his name and counted themselves his friends; and impressed firmly on men's minds the apprehension of a strict and universal judgment and of a final exculpation that would only be gained after an ordeal of unprecedented calamity.

CHAPTER V

THE VIGIL OF THE DAY OF DAYS

So deep was the impression made by the predictions of Christ that from the time of the Apostles onwards for several centuries the expectation of a Second Coming in power held a prominent place in Christian orthodox belief. It was a leading feature in the teaching of Peter and of Paul. It forms the subject of that wonderful series of visions which closes the Canon of the New Testament. It is associated with the names of some of the greatest of the early Fathers of the Church: with Papias, with Irenaeus, with Justin Martyr and with Tertullian. It is found in some of the earliest Christian writings, in the Epistle of Barnabas, in the Testaments of the Twelve Patriarchs, in the Shepherd of Hermas.

In spite of disappointments (for the early believers took in too narrow a sense the promise that the Advent would come to pass soon) the enthusiasm of this hope persisted for some three centuries, and did not begin to wane till the reign of Constantine. Discouraged by the ecclesiastical authorities, it had sunk out of sight by the fifth century, and for a thousand years from that date it appears but little in history.

It never died out of the popular mind, however, and with the Renaissance and the Reformation it once more began to take its old place in Christian belief and thought. As far back as the beginning of the fourteenth century, from the time of Dante and Giotto onward, the art and poetry of Italy depict the Last Judgment in works which are still famous. Orcagna, for example, has a painting of it in the Campo Santo, Pisa, Luca Signorelli in the

Cathedral at Orvieto, Michael Angelo in the Sistine Chapel (1541), while Fra Angelico and Tintoretto dealt with the subject more times than one. Thereafter renderings of the same theme appeared in Germany and elsewhere, Sir E. Burne-Jones's 'Dies Domini' holding the position of a postscript to the long series. Old writers, too, of less distinction than Dante sang of the Last Judgment in verses that are not forgotten:

> Judicabit omnes gentes
> Et salvabit innocentes.
> Dies illa dies vitae
> Dies lucis inauditae
> Qua nox omnis destruetur
> Et mors ipsa morietur.

The English poets of the seventeenth century began to write of the Day that was to be.[1] Henry Vaughan, for example:

> . . . That day, Time's utmost line,
> When all shall perish but what is divine.
> When the great Trumpet's mighty blast shall shake
> The earth's foundations, till the hard Rocks quake,
> And melt like piles of snow, when lightnings move
> Like hail, and the white thrones are set above.
> That day, when sent in glory by the Father
> The Prince of life his blest Elect shall gather;
> Millions of Angels round about him flying,
> While all the kindreds of the earth are crying,
> And he enthron'd upon the clouds shall give
> His last just sentence, who must die, who live.

And John Dryden:

> As from the pow'r of sacred Lays
>   The Spheres began to move,
> And sung the great Creator's praise
>   To all the bless'd above;

So when the last and dreadful hour
This crumbling pageant shall devour,
The TRUMPET shall be heard on high,
The Dead shall live, the Living die,
And MUSICK shall untune the Sky.

In the eighteenth century great thinkers and teachers of
many schools of thought began once more to remember
the expectation of the Return of Christ. One of these was
Bengel, whose work as a scholar is the foundation of all
modern criticism of the text of the New Testament (d.
1752). Another was Sir Isaac Newton; another Charles
Wesley. The period of the French Revolution heightened
the interest in Biblical prophecy. During the first half of
the nineteenth century the general expectation of the
return of Christ played a larger part in general Christian
belief than it had done since the second century, and it
resembled the belief of that early time in that the Advent
was thought to be imminent. Confined almost entirely to
the Protestant communions it was shared by individual
Christians in most, if not all, of the Churches, and aroused
in some sections of Christendom the greatest enthusiasm.
It was proclaimed by bodies such as the Irvingites, and
became the distinctive tenet of various Adventist groups.
It was taught by illustrious divines on the Continent as
well as in England: by Delitzsch and by Godet, as well as
by Archbishop Trench, by Bishop Ellicott, Bishop Ryle,
Canon Fremantle and by Mr. Moody. The literature on
the subject from the time of Bengel's *Exposition of the
Apocalypse* and his *Ordo Temporum a Principio per Periodos
Œconomiae Divinae Historicus atque Propheticus*, grew more
and more voluminous, and interpretations of ancient prophecies more and more various. One scholar fixed the
date of the return as 1785. Bengel gave 1836; William
Miller 1843–4; Cumming 1866. Sometimes the manner,
the place, and the very day of the Second Advent were

determined by calculations of the pious; and on one notorious occasion a concourse of votaries assembled at a designated spot to watch the clouds from which before nightfall a white-robed Messiah was to descend to earth.

The prevalence of this expectation, however, can easily be exaggerated. The Roman and the Orthodox Churches as a whole, and a conservative majority in the more liberal communions, seemed to have remained unaffected.

But the attitude of religious expectancy was not confined to Christendom. It was shared by the followers of other world-religions: by the Buddhists watching for the advent of the fifth Buddha; by the Zoroastrians looking for the Sháh-Bahrám, by the Hindus who so long had waited for the tenth incarnation of Truth called Kalki;* and by Islám looking so eagerly for the twofold Manifestation foretold by Muḥammad.

By the middle of the last century the Christian expectation of the Second Advent had reached its zenith. After that date it began to decline and finally passed out of sight. Even when the sign of the return of the Jews to Palestine was fulfilled so dramatically as to startle the imagination of all acquainted with the predictions of Christ, the former expectancy was not reawakened, and the heart of Christendom was not moved to seek the explanation of so astonishing a phenomenon.

Was this fond and ardent hope then a repetition of the mistake of the second-century Christians? Was all this enthusiasm and activity the product of an ill-ordered and superstitious fancy? Were those who evinced no interest in the stirrings of expectancy, and who were not conscious

---

* 'Vishnu is the god who from time to time becomes incarnate in order to rehabilitate the world . . . The number of these incarnations or "descents" is not fixed . . . At the end of the era he will appear as Kalkin who will inaugurate a new and better age.' (Zaehner, *Hinduism*, p. 120. Cited by Ed.)

of any impulse from on high, proved by the event to be right, and those who watched for the fulfilment of the ancient promise demonstrably and utterly wrong? The world thinks so today; but the Bahá'ís hold an opposite opinion. They maintain that Christian Adventism was not a wild and empty dream, but an intuitive response to a veritable fact. They maintain that the sphere of spiritual thought within which man dwells was charged and sur-charged with the news of the impending Manifestation, and that spiritual minds in touch with this sphere were impressed with an authentic sense of the divine birth that was to be.

It is on record that at the time of the First Coming of Our Lord a mystical warning was floated down from the presence of God upon the spirits of men far and wide. The belief that a great ruler would arise out of the land of Judah was current throughout the East. It is mentioned by Suetonius.[2] It is thought by Tacitus to have been ful-filled by Vespasian who, after the quelling of the Jewish revolt and the destruction of Jerusalem in A.D. 70, cele-brated with his lieutenant Titus a joint triumph for that signal victory. It reached perhaps as far to the west as Rome, where Vergil introduced into one of his Eclogues a mysterious allusion which Christians have always inter-preted as a direct reference to the birth of Christ, and its inspiration vouchsafed an exact knowledge of the truth to watchers as far apart as the aged Simeon in Jerusalem and the Wise Men in some unnamed region towards the rising of the stars.

However widespread and constant that belief, it did not lead the compatriots of Vergil or of the Magi, nor any other Gentile people to look for an epiphany of God or to recognise the World Deliverer in the prophet of Galilee. Even the Jews themselves, in spite of their extraordinary privileges, in spite of the special guidance of their history and their Scripture, and though their land was designated as the centre of the general expectation, remained as blind to the Divine Event as any of those whom they despised as unillumined foreigners and heathens.

The failure of the Jews to appreciate the importance of the Lord Christ is compared by the Bahá'ís to the failure of the world at the present time to appreciate the importance of Bahá'u'lláh and his teachings. The reasons for the insensibility of mankind today are said to be of the same character as those which caused a similar insensibility at the beginning of the Era. In the case of the Jews, prejudice and traditionalism had warped the judgment of the people and their leaders and had led in particular to a profound misinterpretation of prophecy. Predictions were taken not in a spiritual or in a figurative way but in a sense that was merely literal and sometimes childish, so that instead of being a light to guide to the truth they became a screen to shut off all vision of it.

So significant did 'Abdu'l-Bahá consider this misunderstanding that he added to Dr. Esslemont's *Bahá'u'lláh and the New Era* a special statement of his own on the subject.

When Christ appeared, twenty centuries ago, although the Jews were eagerly awaiting His coming, and prayed every day, with tears, saying: 'O God, hasten the revelation of the Messiah,' yet when the Sun of Truth dawned, they denied Him and rose against Him with the greatest enmity, and eventually crucified that divine Spirit, the Word of God, and named Him Beelzebub, the evil one, as is recorded in the Gospel. The reason for this was that they said: 'The revelation of Christ, according to the clear text of the Torah, will be attested by certain signs, and so long as these signs have not appeared, whoso layeth claim to be a Messiah is an imposter. Among these signs is this, that the

Messiah should come from an unknown place, yet we all know this man's house in Nazareth, and can any good thing come out of Nazareth? The second sign is that He shall rule with a rod of iron, that is, He must act with the sword, but this Messiah has not even a wooden staff. Another of the conditions and signs is this: He must sit upon the throne of David and establish David's sovereignty. Now, far from being enthroned, this man has not even a mat to sit on. Another of the conditions is this: the promulgation of all the laws of the Torah; yet this man has abrogated these laws, and has even broken the sabbath day, although it is the clear text of the Torah that whosoever layeth claim to prophethood and revealeth miracles and breaketh the sabbath day, must be put to death. Another of the signs is this, that in His reign justice will be so advanced that righteousness and well-doing will extend from the human even to the animal world—the snake and the mouse will share one hole, and the eagle and the partridge one nest, the lion and the gazelle shall dwell in one pasture, and the wolf and the kid shall drink from one fountain. Yet now, injustice and tyranny have waxed so great in His time that they have crucified Him! Another of the conditions is this, that in the days of the Messiah the Jews will prosper and triumph over all the peoples of the world, but now they are living in the utmost abasement and servitude in the Empire of the Romans. Then how can this be the Messiah promised in the Torah?'

In this wise did they object to that Sun of Truth, although that Spirit of God was indeed the One promised in the Torah. But as they did not understand the meaning of these signs, they crucified the Word of God. Now the Bahá'ís hold that the recorded signs did come to pass in the Manifestation of Christ, although

not in the sense which the Jews understood, the description in the Torah being allegorical. For instance,
among the signs is that of sovereignty. The Bahá'ís say
that the sovereignty of Christ was a heavenly, divine,
everlasting sovereignty, not a Napoleonic sovereignty
that vanisheth in a short time. For well-nigh two
thousand years this sovereignty of Christ hath been
established, and until now it endureth, and to all
eternity that holy Being will be exalted upon an everlasting throne.

In like manner all the other signs have been made
manifest, but the Jews did not understand. Although
nearly twenty centuries have elapsed since Christ appeared with divine splendour, yet the Jews are still
awaiting the coming of the Messiah and regard themselves as true and Christ as false.[3]

In a parallel manner, the Bahá'ís believe the millenarians
of the last century, while showing a remarkable delicacy
of spiritual touch, were robbed of the first fruits of their
intuitiveness by a misapprehension of the meaning of
their Scriptures. By taking, for example, the statement
that Christ would return in a cloud in a purely literal
sense, they missed the warning conveyed by the allegory
of a cloud (as explained in Bahá'u'lláh's *Book of Certitude*)
and brought dire confusion upon themselves by imagin-
ing that Jesus would descend bodily out of the strato-
sphere in a floating fog. The whole fact of the personal
return of Christ indeed was misunderstood by them
through their lack of information as to the principle of
God's recurrent manifestations. They did not look for a
return analogous to that of Elijah in John the Baptist or
Abraham in Moses. They did not consider that he who
said, 'I will come again,' also said 'Before Abraham was,
I am.' Their minds were not set upon a re-manifestation

in another human form of that eternal and unchanging Essence which Christ called 'I'; but merely on a reappearance out of the sky of that very self-same being who previously had been born among them of the Virgin Mary. Furthermore, the Bahá'ís assert that in the Bible, both Old and New Testaments, as in the Scriptures of other world-religions, the commands and ordinances of the Most High are given in plain language and have no concealed meaning; but on the other hand, the 'things kept secret from the foundation of the world', mysteries of the future and predictions of the coming of the Kingdom, are set forth in symbol or parable with a deeper meaning hidden underneath the literal significance of the words.

These prophecies, therefore, admit of misinterpretation; and Holy Writ contained warnings of the difficulty of reading them aright. In his *Bahá'í Proofs* Mírzá Abu'l-Faḍl, a renowned Bahá'í scholar, deals at length with this question of Bible prophecy (pp. 198–214) and points out that while predictions as to the last Day are numerous in all the Holy Books yet these Books definitely assert that by the decree of God no one will be able to open and unveil the true meaning of these predictions till the Great Day actually breaks, and that even at that late date the right interpretation will be withheld from all save those whom God elects.

He quotes as texts in proof Isaiah vi. 10–12.

Make the heart of this people fat, and make their ears heavy, and shut their eyes; lest they see with their eyes, and hear with their ears, and understand with their heart, and convert, and be healed. Then said I, Lord, how long? And he answered, Until the cities be wasted without inhabitant, and the houses without man, and the land be utterly desolate, And the Lord have removed men far away, and *there be* a great forsaking in the midst of the land.

and two passages from Daniel xii:

But thou, O Daniel, shut up the words, and seal the book, *even* to the time of the end: many shall run to and fro, and knowledge shall be increased. (4.)

And he said, Go thy way, Daniel: for the words *are* closed up and sealed till the time of the end. Many shall be purified, and made white, and tried; but the wicked shall do wickedly: and none of the wicked shall understand; but the wise shall understand. (9, 10.)

As in Christendom, so throughout the rest of the world. The universal expectation of an august theophany was vitiated by misunderstandings and led to no good result. A rigid traditionalism cramped the souls of men. No organised religion in any quarter of the globe seems to have believed that the coming Prophet would demand radical reforms and lift the people to a higher level of thought and conduct than that with which they had contented themselves in the past. Every religion looked for a Vindicator who should be exclusively its own, who should justify its dogmas, reinforce its institutions and exalt it to a position of complete and unchallengeable supremacy over the erroneous faiths of the rest of mankind.

The world's unanimity, therefore, in looking for a Divine Advent was not so complete as to suggest that when the Deliverer actually appeared all the communions of all races would be at one in acclaiming him. Far otherwise. Not only had each of the great religions drawn in rough outline its own distinctive picture of the Messiah, but some of these religions were themselves subdivided into numerous sects each of which had prepared the Messiah's portrait in yet smaller and more exclusive detail. However ready, therefore, to accommodate himself to the predilections of man the Divine Teacher might prove to be, it is evident that he could by no possibility gratify the expectations of more than a minute proportion of the human race and must at the same time keenly disappoint the hopes of all the other millions of mankind. On the other hand, if the Holy Prophet should come (as all Holy Prophets had done before him), disregarding all human preconceptions, bearing a new Name, bringing a new Book, he would be confronted by the denial of every section of every extant religion. His acceptance would be secured through the private judgment of independent individuals.

The primary blame for the disregard paid to the teaching of Bahá'u'lláh rests, according to the Bahá'ís, with the votaries of one religion in particular: with the Muslims. Had Islám been less unworthy of the great privilege vouchsafed it; had Sháh and Sulṭán not headed the forces of obscurantism, the plight of mankind today (believe the Bahá'ís) would be less sad, and the outlook would be less menacing. Had not that mirror of divine perfection, the Supreme Spokesman and Vicegerent of God, been held in prison during the whole period of his Manifestation he would have been able, instead of addressing the rulers of the West by letter (which he did), to visit their dominions himself and to have lent to the Declaration of his Mission the immediate authority and impressiveness of a more than imperial personality. Had such an ordinary freedom been allowed him, the present delay in the recognition of the New Jerusalem would have been avoided and the nations would have been saved an immensity of suffering.

Muḥammadanism was the last of the world-religions, and it contained a number of predictions which indicated clearly that it was to be the seat and centre of the universally expected Avatar. These prophecies were in some respects more definite and detailed than any in other faiths. They showed that the coming Advent was to be twofold —there were to be two Manifestors of the Very Self of God; and also that when these appeared they would introduce far-reaching changes in the order of Church and State, bringing a new social system and a new teaching. All the sects of Islám accepted the former prophecy; but most did not expect a new book.

Furthermore, reliable traditions (ḥadíth) of sayings ascribed to the Prophet Muḥammad made one forecast which by its subject stands apart from all, or almost all, the others, because it concerns not so much the spiritual manifestation itself or its effects, as the temple, the lamp, the particular human body which was to be brought into being to serve as the shrine for the manifestation.

The predictions of Christ had been many and remarkable. But Christ had not named the religion within the confines of which his return would take place. In these prophecies he adverted once only to the Christian faith, and this reference was a warning that he would cast out as workers of iniquity some who used his name. Nor did he designate any point about the locality or the corporeal element of his return. On the other hand, Muslim traditions clearly foretold that the next Mirror of the Godhead, the Qá'im, would appear within the fold of Islám, and would be one of Muḥammad's own lineal descendants. Because of this well-known and important prognostication the blood-descendants of the Prophet were with the greater care marked out in Islám; and all who claimed the honour of such ancestry were, in the Shí'ah sect, styled 'Siyyid' and were publicly distinguished from all less fortunate Muslims by wearing a turban of green.

A declaration so clear narrowed the field of search, and made the task of recognising the new Qá'im a simpler undertaking. Had the adherents of other faiths heeded this prophecy, what errors and what calamities would have been avoided! But even on Islám itself the kindly help and counsel of its Prophet was wasted. Though they had these pronouncements and a hundred others hardly less illuminating to aid them, the Muslims made no use of their Prophet's assistance, and when the hour of fulfilment came rejected without hesitation the stainless radiant Siyyid in whose person met all the signs of divinity that Muḥammad had set forth.

The name of him who was chosen as the new High-Prophet was Mírzá 'Alí-Muḥammad. He was the first of the two expected Messengers, and his function was to open the way in men's hearts for the still greater Messenger that was to follow. He assumed in consequence the descriptive title of 'the Gate', drawing attention thereby to the preparatory nature of his work. He was to Bahá'u'lláh as John the Baptist was to Christ. But inasmuch as the approaching Theophany was to mark the culmination of all human history he himself held the station of an independent High-Prophet and was endowed, as Muḥammad had been, with the fullness of divine authority. Like any other High-Prophet, he did not come among men unheralded. Fifty-one years before his Declaration there arose a certain Aḥmad-i-Aḥsá'í, a man of saintly character and high intelligence, who began with tact and caution the task of preparing the Muslims for the Advent of the Qá'im. Great as was his reputation and influence he did not find amongst those who listened one solitary person able to appreciate the import of his message, till after twenty years he was approached by a young man, Siyyid Káẓim, whom he at once recognised as a pure and spiritual soul. He took Káẓim as his comrade and fellow-labourer, and for about ten years the two worked together until Aḥmad died in his early eighties.

From the beginning Aḥmad knew and proclaimed that

a double epiphany of God was impending, and that the approaching Day would be one of dazzling magnificence. Though he never met the Báb in the flesh, nor yet Bahá-'u'lláh, he drew particular attention to the city of Shíráz, the place from which the voice of the Báb was to be heard; and when men were astonished at the greatness of his enthusiasm over this city, he said, 'Wonder not, for ere long the secret of my words will be made manifest to you. Among you there shall be a number who will live to behold the glory of a Day which the prophets of old have yearned to witness.'[5]

He did not himself live, however, to see the dawning of that Great Day. His task completed, he died at an advanced age some eighteen years before the Declaration of the Báb,[6] and was buried near the grave of Muḥammad in the city of Medina.

It was reserved for Káẓim to meet the Báb in person, to recognise and definitely acknowledge him as the Qá'im, and though refusing to publish his name, yet to portray him so distinctly as to leave little room for uncertainty. He said that the Advent was at hand, and the Prophet himself in their midst: 'You behold Him with your own eyes, and yet recognise Him not!' Pressed with questions, he would say, 'He is of noble lineage. He is a descendant of the Prophet of God, of the family of Háshim. He is young in age, and is possessed of innate knowledge . . . He is of medium height, abstains from smoking, and is of extreme devoutness and piety.'[7]

Teaching at all times the twofold nature of the coming Manifestation, towards the close of his life he emphasised this with greater force and insistence. He bade his more earnest followers leave all they possessed, and scatter far and wide to seek that hidden King of Kings, the unrevealed Overlord of the Last Day, whose privilege it was to decide who should become the champions of the Báb.

Be firm [he said to them] till the day when He will choose you as the companions and the heroic supporters of the promised Qá'im. Well is it with every one of you who will quaff the cup of martyrdom in His path ... Verily I say, after the Qá'im the Qayyúm will be made manifest [i.e. the Báb and Bahá'u'lláh]. For when the star of the Former has set, the sun of the beauty of Ḥusayn will rise and illuminate the whole world. Then will be unfolded in all its glory the 'mystery' and the 'secret' spoken of by Shaykh Aḥmad, who has said: 'The mystery of this Cause must needs be made manifest, and the secret of this message must needs be divulged.' ... O my beloved companions! How great, how very great, is the Cause! How exalted the station to which I summon you! How great the mission for which I have trained and prepared you! Gird up the loins of endeavour, and fix your gaze upon His promise. I pray to God graciously to assist you to weather the storms of tests and trials which must needs beset you, to enable you to emerge, unscathed and triumphant, from their midst, and to lead you to your high destiny.[8]

CHAPTER VI

THE GATE OF THE DAWN

A few months from that day on which in America the adherents of William Miller stood looking up to heaven to catch the first glimpse of the Saviour returning in glory among the clouds, on the other side of the world the Báb gave forth the Declaration of his Sacred Mission and began his appointed work of preparing mankind for the dawning of the Last Day and the advent of its Lord.

Born October 20th, 1819, he was at the time of his Declaration a youth of twenty-five years of age. Of those eager active souls whom he quickly gathered about him to raise the standard of the Cause of God, not a few were, like himself, in the prime of their young manhood. Perhaps the flame of their youthfulness helped to animate the Bábí movement with that spirit of daring and adventure and indomitable courage which has helped to spread its fame far among the nations. Certainly the radiant charm and sweetness of its hero which made him seem Love's avatar, and that instinctive power which was his of drawing forth from all who opened to him their hearts a passionate devotion which shrank from no sacrifice—certainly these qualities and the heinousness of the priestly hate that martyred him, have given to the brief sad chronicle of his career a tragic beauty which makes it one of the most poignant episodes in the history of the religious world.

From the beginning it was the sole purpose of the Báb to prepare men for the advent of Bahá'u'lláh. In 1843, the year before his Declaration, he had in a dream a strange symbolic experience, and on his awakening he felt that the Spirit of God had come upon him and possessed him and he saw unfolded before his eyes all the glories of the great Revelation that was to be. The sacred title which he assumed, the Gate, signified that his mission was introductory: its intent was to open into men's hearts a passage through which this mighty Revelation could enter.

The similitude of 'the Gate' was not unfamiliar to Christians. Christ had used it in one of the most beautiful and favourite parables, and had applied it in a peculiarly enigmatic manner. He had strangely presented himself in one and the same parable under two quite different images. 'I am the Gate,' he said, and again, 'I am he who enters by the Gate.' He went on to explain that he who entered by the Gate and not in any other way was the True Shepherd and would be followed by those who knew the divine voice, the divine word.

The title 'Gate' was yet more familiar to the Muḥammadans, and the Báb took care that it should not be misrepresented nor misunderstood. 'The condemnation of God be upon him who regards me either as a representative of the Imám or the gate thereof,' he declared publicly in the Mosque at Shíráz in 1845.[1]

He was the gate of a wholly new Advent. In his first and most important book he adverted to his Lord: 'O Thou Remnant of God! I have sacrificed myself wholly for Thee; I have accepted curses for thy sake, and have yearned for naught but martyrdom in the path of Thy love.'[2] While paying the greatest honour to the Apostles of Jesus, he instructed the 'Letters of the Living' whom he sent forth that even the Day of the Apostles was not as illustrious as that which was about to break. He knew well that it would be universal, compassing the whole world; and the thought of his work for it was so precious that it illumined and sweetened even his most intimate sorrows. His prayer of self-consecration over the dead body of his little son concluded with the words:

> Endue with Thy grace My life-blood which I yearn to shed in Thy path. Cause it to water and nourish the seed of Thy Faith. Endow it with Thy celestial potency, that this infant seed of God may soon germinate in the hearts of men, that it may thrive and prosper, that it may grow to become a mighty tree, beneath the shadow of which all the peoples and kindreds of the earth may gather. Answer Thou My prayer, O God, and fulfil My most cherished desire.[3]

Nor was it the teaching of Bahá'u'lláh alone that was to girdle the earth. The influence of the Báb reached far to the east and to the west—westward to the Adventists of Europe and America, and eastward likewise, as appears from the incident of the dervish whom the spell of the Báb drew to his side from distant India. This pilgrim told how when he was a nawab in India he had seen the Báb in a vision and had yielded up his heart at once. The Báb fixed his gaze upon him and bade him leave his native land and come on foot to Persia where in Chihríq he would attain his heart's desire. The dervish, giving up his exalted post and laying aside his gorgeous attire, travelled to Persia as bidden, and finding the Báb in the prison of Chihríq, acknowledged his prophethood and mission and afterward returned on foot to India as he had come, to spread there by the Báb's command the Tidings of the New Revelation.

From childhood the Báb was remarkable for his natural piety, his stainless life and his intuitive understanding of spiritual things. Those who knew him speak of the engaging grace of his manner, of his kindliness, his courtesy, his dignity. The most humble and the most simple of men, he combined serenity with eagerness of spirit; and none could mistake his courage, his independence or the masterful quality of his character and will.

His calling was that of a merchant; and his conception of business morality was not only much above that of the corrupt and venal people among whom he worked but was such as is not always found in the market-places of Christendom.

The following account of one of the Báb's business transactions is recorded by Nabíl.

A certain man confided to His care a trust, requesting Him to dispose of it at a fixed price. When the Báb sent him the value of that article, the man found that the sum which he had been offered considerably exceeded the limit which he had fixed. He immediately wrote to the Báb, requesting Him to explain the reason. The Báb replied: 'What I have sent you is entirely your due. There is not a single farthing in excess of what is your right. There was a time when the trust you had delivered to Me had attained this value. Failing to sell it at that price, I now feel it My duty to offer you the whole of that sum.' However much the Báb's client entreated Him to receive back the sum in excess, the Báb persisted in refusing.[4]

On the other hand, the Báb taught that it was wrong to permit a tradesman to ask more than the fair price for an article. Once when he was in prison he asked that some honey should be purchased for him. This was done, but at a figure which he considered exorbitant. He refused to accept the honey, and said:

Honey of a superior quality could no doubt have been purchased at a lower price. I who am your example
D

have been a merchant by profession. It behoves you in all your transactions to follow in My way. You must neither defraud your neighbour nor allow him to defraud you. Such was the way of your Master. The shrewdest and ablest of men were unable to deceive Him, nor did He on His part choose to act ungenerously towards the meanest and most helpless of creatures.[5]

So long as the Báb appeared as a merchant and an ordinary citizen, he enjoyed the warm friendship and regard of all. When, however, he declared to Ḥusayn, 'I am the Báb, the Gate of God'; when he made a similar declaration to Mírzá Muḥíṭ in Mecca and delivered the Message of God to the Meccan Sherif, calling on him to embrace the Cause of God; when in the presence of the heir to the Persian throne and the assembled dignitaries of Tabríz he publicly proclaimed, 'I am the Promised One, whose name you have for a thousand years invoked'; when he wrote to Muḥammad Sháh, 'I am the Primal Point from which have been generated all created things . . . I am the Countenance of God, whose splendour can never be obscured, the light of God whose radiance can never fade . . .';[6] when with speeding pen he poured forth epistles, commentaries and other writings with such profusion that in the end—so he stated—the total volume amounted to '500,000 verses'; when he sent forth eighteen chosen messengers to prepare the way of the Cause, and when, through his own influence and theirs, multitudes in many districts were stirred by the new teaching: when he began to manifest such activities as these, the envious hierophants of Persia took strong measures to check and to reverse the current of popular feeling and to bring the new prophet and his works to naught.

The teaching was in itself such as no lover of God or of mankind could object to.

> . . . Babism [wrote Lord Curzon in his *Persia and the Persian Question* (p. 502)] may be defined as a creed of charity and almost of common humanity. Brotherly love, kindness to children, courtesy combined with dignity, sociability, hospitality, freedom from bigotry, friendliness even to Christians, are included in its tenets.

The spiritual purity and exaltation of the Báb's Cause may be gathered from the address he gave to his apostles as he sent them out to spread his Gospel throughout Persia. It runs in part as follows:

> O My beloved friends! You are the bearers of the name of God in this Day. You have been chosen as the repositories of His mystery. It behoves each one of you to manifest the attributes of God, and to exemplify by your deeds and words the signs of His righteousness, His power and glory. The very members of your body must bear witness to the loftiness of your purpose, the integrity of your life, the reality of your faith and the exalted character of your devotion. For verily I say, this is the Day spoken of by God in His Book: 'On that day will We set a seal upon their mouths; yet shall their hands speak unto Us, and their feet shall bear witness to that which they shall have done.' . . . You are the witnesses of the Dawn of the promised Day of God. You are the partakers of the mystic chalice of His Revelation. Gird up the loins of endeavour . . . Purge your hearts of worldly desires, and let angelic virtues be your adorning . . . The days when idle worship was deemed sufficient are ended.

The time is come when naught but the purest motive, supported by deeds of stainless purity, can ascend to the throne of the Most High and be acceptable unto Him . . . You have been called to this station; you will attain to it, only if you arise to trample beneath your feet every earthly desire, and endeavour to become those 'honoured servants of His who speak not till He hath spoken, and who do His bidding' . . . Beseech the Lord your God to grant that no earthly entanglements, no worldly affections, no ephemeral pursuits, may tarnish the purity, or embitter the sweetness, of that grace which flows through you. I am preparing you for the advent of a mighty Day. Exert your utmost endeavour that, in the world to come, I, who am now instructing you, may, before the mercy-seat of God, rejoice in your deeds and glory in your achievements . . . Scatter throughout the length and breadth of this land, and, with steadfast feet and sanctified hearts, prepare the way for His coming. Heed not your weaknesses and frailty; fix your gaze upon the invincible power of the Lord, your God, the Almighty . . . Arise in His name, put your trust wholly in Him, and be assured of ultimate victory.[7]

Owing to the shortness of his life, and to his being immured at a distance from his followers for four years out of the six of his ministry, he was prevented from directing the practice of his precepts and from explaining as he would have wished the changes which these precepts involved. That which actuated the faith of the early Bábís was less the acceptance of a new standard of conduct or a new philosophy of life than a personal devotion to the Báb and an enthusiastic belief in his prophethood.

The teaching of the Báb, like his character, was beautiful and attractive; but his function of making ready a

way for the advent of Bahá'u'lláh combined with the
abject degradation of the Persian Church, made him
appear as in the first place a breaker of idols, an assailant
of abuses, a remover of obsolete but cherished laws and
traditions. As the Jews of old accused Jesus of 'changing
the customs which Moses delivered unto them' so with
not less indignation did the Muslims accuse the Báb of
altering the customs commanded by Muḥammad.

Those who were masters in Islám proved themselves
tragically incapable of perceiving his greatness, of recognising the reality of his mission or of appreciating the
value of the gifts which he sought to bestow on them and
on all their countrymen. It was their habit to regard all
matters in relation to themselves only, and their view of
their personal interests was of the most narrow, trivial and
sordid kind. The spirit of the Faith which Muḥammad
and the Imáms had taught and lived had long since van-
ished. As Aḥmad and Kázim had sadly testified, sincerity
of devotion was hard if not impossible to find. The forms
of religion survived and the apparatus of worship was
still treasured; but in spite of much self-righteousness
and parade reality had gone. The clerics of Islám had
worked over and interpreted the teachings of their
Prophet and had deftly moulded it to fit exactly their personal wishes and illusions. In their hands it had been
crystallised into the law of an institution which encouraged every form of rapacity and oppression. The officers
of State and Church were enabled to follow in the name
of their Prophet their own dark pleasures, unillumined
by any love for God and undeterred by any fear of his
vengeance. The reforms of the Báb challenged the cor-
ruptions and the hypocrisies of the time; and when his
energetic measures rapidly spread his influence far and
wide, the forces of the government were at once mobil-
ised against him. From that moment the story of the

Bábí Cause becomes one of darkening tragedy, until at last the light of love seems to be quenched in the dust of death for ever.

The authorities at first tried to bring the Báb into ridicule and contempt and to intimidate him by cruel punishment. Failing in this effort, they shut him up in a fortress, forbidding communication with the outer world. His followers were denounced as foes of State and Church. They were subjected to many forms of ostracism, were despoiled, beaten, and in some instances put to death. In three districts the persecution became so severe that the Bábís, driven at last to desperation, took up arms in defence of their lives. In Nayríz and in Zanján they occupied military posts which were lying virtually untenanted. In Mázindarán under the leadership of Mullá Husayn and Quddús they built themselves a rude but well-contrived and substantial fortress. In these positions (by a movement wholly spontaneous and unconcerted and pressed on them in each case by local violence) three several groups of Bábís established themselves and having procured what small arms they could, awaited peaceably the onset of their assailants. That which follows is surely one of the most extraordinary campaigns in the chronicle of irregular warfare. One is not likely to find in any age a more conspicuous example of the prodigious power of sheer morale or of the literal truth of the poet's statement that 'My strength is as the strength of ten because my heart is pure.' The story disproves the well-known maxim of the great conqueror that God is on the side of the biggest battalions; for certainly in this instance, he was on the side of the few who defied the many, of the weak who routed the strong. A professional soldier would describe the Bábís as an 'armed mob', for they were composed of civilians of both sexes and of all ages: some had left their shops, some their pulpits, but none had come from the camp. Their numbers were in each case small—in Mázindarán only some three hundred. Against each of these three companies were marshalled brigades of the choicest troops of the Sháh consisting of cavalry and artillery as well as infantry, fully equipped for battle and led by distinguished officers. The Bábís were surrounded by their foes and subjected to the privations of a siege. They suffered great hardship, and were for days at a time reduced to subsisting on nothing better than boiled grass. Yet their faith remained unshaken, their courage undaunted, their enthusiasm undimmed. They took the greatest care to stand strictly on the defensive and to leave aggression to their opponents. Many times, however, they anticipated an impending attack by a sally from the fort, and a few hundred or a few score Bábís would break the enemy's line, overturning their cannon, and driving them headlong in disorder. As soon, however, as they had made the threatened attack impossible, the Bábís would stay their pursuit, lower their weapons and return to their fort, there to enjoy as best they might a respite from the struggle till once more the enemy were reinforced and made ready for a new onset.

Quddús, during the last days of the siege of Mázindarán and a short time before his own martyrdom, made the following declaration:

Never since our occupation of this fort have we under any circumstances attempted to direct any offensive against our opponents. Not until they unchained their attack upon us did we arise to defend our lives. Had we cherished the ambition of waging holy war against them, had we harboured the least intention of achieving ascendancy through the power of our arms over the unbelievers, we should not, until this day, have remained besieged within these walls. The force of our arms would have by now, as was the case with the companions of Muḥammad in days past, convulsed the nations of the earth and prepared them for the acceptance of our Message. Such is not the way, however, which we have chosen to tread. Ever since we repaired to this fort, our sole, our unalterable purpose has been the vindication, by our deeds and by our readiness to shed our blood in the path of our Faith, of the exalted character of our mission. The hour is fast approaching when we shall be able to consummate this task.[8]

This extraordinary conflict between a handful of beleaguered Bábís and the encircling regiments of the Sháh continued in each instance for months. No losses, no suffering weakened the defence, nor did the thought of saving their lives by any kind of recantation or compromise enter the minds of the besieged. When not engaged in self-defence, they spent their time in the study of the Scripture, chanting with unabated fervour the praises of their Lord, the Báb, and pouring forth thanksgivings to God for the heaven-born felicity which had been poured into their hearts. In Mázindarán, and also in Nayríz, the two commanders-in-chief of the forces of the government, growing weary of the humiliating defeats to which their troops were subjected, at last ostensibly yielded to the Bábís and (under the most solemn oath) promised them safe conduct and freedom from future molestation. But as soon as the besieged had come out from the shelter of their walls, had laid aside their arms and separated, they ordered a general massacre, which was duly carried out by the troops and the populace, not without the accompaniment of torture. In Zanján the numbers engaged were larger, and the conflict more prolonged. In the tenth month, the Bábís having lost nearly a thousand men, including their leader, Ḥujjat, the Sháh's general flung his troops against the fort in a determined assault, and by sheer weight of numbers drove the Bábís before him into the neighbouring houses where they stood once more at bay. Seeing the position was untenable, and being encumbered with many women and wounded, those of the Bábís who still could bear arms made a last charge upon the troops, being resolved to die fighting. Some were killed, some were captured, and all resistance ended.

Thus were lost to the Cause of Reform in Persia many of the most earnest followers of the Báb, including four of his ablest leaders, Mullá Ḥusayn, the first to acknowledge the Báb, and known therefore by the title of 'the Gate of the Gate', and Vaḥíd, and Ḥujjat, and Quddús, who was esteemed as nearer to the Báb than any other of his apostles.

But the wanton sacrifice of all these lives was not the only nor the greatest crime of the obscurantists of that time and land. To this they added another more heinous yet. They felt that from his remote and lonely prison among the northern hills the splendour of the Báb still shone afar, troubling their darkness and lighting the onward path of his followers. So long as he lived, their misdeeds might be exposed and their power destroyed. The force of his presence, though they did not doubt it was diabolical, was yet so winning that if he succeeded at any time in his efforts to gain an interview with the Sháh, he might win his Majesty's favour and supplant them in their position of privilege near the royal person. They could not rest secure till the Báb was dead.

Often had the Báb prayed for the glory of martyrdom. Often had he with exultation foretold his prayer would not go ungranted. To some he had indicated the approach of the destined day. Now, aware that the time was at hand, he collected all the documents in his possession and placing them with a few personal treasures in a coffer sent them all by a trusty messenger to his Lord Bahá'u'lláh.

A few days later, he was (by an arbitrary act of the Grand Vizir without any colour of law or justice) summoned from his prison to Tabríz. There on July 9th, 1850, in the presence of ten thousand people who crowded windows and roofs to behold the spectacle, he attained the goal of his dearest hopes, and, having ever offered up to his Beloved all that life contained, now crowned his offerings with that of life itself.

His body, riddled with bullets, save for the face which was but little marked, was recovered by his disciples, and under the direction of Bahá'u'lláh, hidden in a place of safety. Ultimately it was conveyed to the Holy Land and now lies in a mausoleum on the slopes of Mount Carmel.

The martyrdom of the Báb and of so many of his ablest and most eager followers, left the main body of the survivors for the moment bewildered and despondent. But there remained those among them who were able to face the emergency, to instil courage into drooping hearts, and to carry forward the work which the Báb's enemies thought must with his disappearance sink speedily and for ever into oblivion.

The progress of the Cause had from the beginning been due not a little to the efforts of a lady of wealth and noble birth, known as Qurratu'l-'Ayn (Solace of the Eyes) or Ṭáhirih (the Pure) whose genius has made her one of the most brilliant figures in the early history of the Bahá'í movement. Professor Browne writes of her as follows:

> The appearance of such a woman . . . is in any country and any age a rare phenomenon, but in such a country as Persia it is a prodigy—nay, almost a miracle. Alike in virtue of her marvellous beauty, her

rare intellectual gifts, her fervid eloquence, her fearless devotion, and her glorious martyrdom, she stands forth incomparable and immortal amidst her country-women. Had the Bábí religion no other claim to greatness, this were sufficient—that it produced a heroine like Ḳurratu'l-'Ayn.[9]

Other impartial spectators have written of her with an enthusiasm as warm. She was included by the Báb among his chosen Apostles or Letters of the Living: the only woman in their ranks. So clear was her vision, so deep her faith in God, that she counted the earth and its concerns as dust, and threw all to the winds that she might with a pure heart give herself utterly to the Cause of the Báb. Her personal charm, her intellectual supremacy and her radiant confidence gained for her an immense influence with her countrymen, which had reached its height in the summer of 1852. Nabíl, in his chronicle, tells of the 'affection and high esteem in which she was held by the leading women of the capital' and how her house 'was besieged by her women admirers, who thronged her doors, eager to enter her presence and to seek the benefit of her knowledge'.[10]

But the consolidation of the Báb's work at this time and the extension of his teachings was due pre-eminently to the enthusiasm and the ability of Bahá'u'lláh who set himself the task of reviving the energies of the Báb's followers and of organising and directing their activities. He gave them the guidance of which in their consternation they stood so much in need. He cheered their spirits, deepened their conviction and inspired them with a forti-tude steadfast enough to endure the trials with which so soon they were to be confronted.

The adversaries of the Báb were thus compelled to watch in astonishment and dismay the steady progress of the Cause which they thought they had destroyed. They saw it spread on every side, and even percolate into foreign lands. Determined to annihilate it, they waited with what patience they might for an opportunity to arise. In the early autumn of 1852 their chance came. Two young Bábís, driven to frenzy by the death of the Báb, determined to take revenge, and made an attempt to shoot the Sháh. The youths were obscure and irresponsible, and the imbecility of their enterprise was shown by the fact that they charged their pistol, not with a bullet, but with small shot. They failed. The Sháh was but slightly wounded, and the assailant who fired the shot was lynched on the spot. But the attempt gave the authorities the opportunity for which so long they had been looking. They were able to represent the crime, though it was repugnant to all the principles of the Báb, and was condemned with horror by every Bábí, as a proof that the Bábí Faith was a subversive creed, and had for its aim the wrecking of the realm. Inflamed themselves with apprehension and fanatical hate, and resolved not to lose the excuse for extirpating the odious faith once and for all, they worked up the populace to a storm of rage and turned them loose upon the Bábís in a campaign of wild and indiscriminate persecution. Throughout the length and breadth of the land Bábís, whatever their age or sex, were treated as outlaws and without inquiry handed over to the mercies of their adversaries. Indignities, crimes of all kinds, and death were visited upon them; and to increase the terror their punishments were made as public, as spectacular and as atrocious as possible. No citizen who at that period walked out into the streets of a city could tell what scenes of carnage and of torture he might be called upon to witness. No Bábí wife or mother holding her infant to her breast could tell at what moment she might not be haled from her hiding-place to suffer any fate a ruffian soldier or blood-thirsty mob might choose to inflict. Executions were carried out indifferently in square, street or market-place and took what form the carnival spirit of the doomsters might at the moment devise.

By a barbarous arrangement, surely without parallel, the Grand Vizir directed that the responsibility for the martyrdoms should be divided out among the departments of state as well as the chief professions and callings of the realm. All these were to participate directly in the executions. One Bábí victim was assigned to the Home Office and was publicly killed by its members. Another Bábí was cut to pieces by the Foreign Secretary and his assistants. Another by the clergy; another by the artillery; another by the infantry; others by the cavalry, the nobility, the merchants or other bodies or guilds. The Sháh himself, through his representative, the Steward of the Household, assisted by minor officials, carried out the martyrdom of the believer allotted to him. Even foreigners connected with the Court were involved in this revolting scheme. One of them, Dr. Cloquet, the Sháh's French physician, was actually asked to take his share in the massacre and kill a Bábí with his own hand: which, of course, he declined to do. Others were compelled as part of their regular duty to witness scenes the bare description of which makes a European's blood run cold with horror. An Austrian officer, Captain von Goumoens, who was in the Sháh's service at the time, narrated how Bábís were brought to the place of the attempt on the Sháh's life, how their eyes were gouged out and they were forced to eat their own amputated ears; how the bazaar would be lighted by Bábís whose bodies were all blood and fire because in breasts, shoulders and backs deep wounds had been made to serve as sconces for lighted candles which burned down to the flesh and flickered in their living sockets; how fresh tortures would follow—how (he himself had seen it, often, too often!) the executioners would 'skin the soles of the Bábís' feet, soak the wounds in boiling oil, shoe the foot like the hoof of a horse, and compel the victim to run. No cry escaped from the victim's breast; the torment is endured in dark silence by the numbed sensation of the fanatic; now he must run; the body cannot endure what the soul has endured; he falls. Give him the *coup de grâce*! Put him out of his pain! No! The executioner swings the whip, and—I myself have had to witness it—the unhappy victim of hundredfold tortures runs!'[11]

Bahá'u'lláh was arrested and flung into a noisome dungeon along with some other Bábís and a number of criminals, to await sentence. One by one the Bábís were taken out and executed; but before the turn of Bahá'u'lláh arrived, an edict was issued that no more Bábís should be put to death without inquiry. Bahá'u'lláh's innocence being established, his life was spared, and having been degraded from his high estate and despoiled of his vast possessions, he was condemned to exile. In January, 1853, with his family and a band of devoted followers, he left his beloved native land for ever.

Thus did Persia scorn and reject those chosen sons of hers who might have lifted her from her insignificance and restored to her more than her ancient splendour and renown. Thus did the Muslim hierarchy cast out the teachers who would have purified Islám and made it the starting-place of a religious revival that in a few years would have poured its light around the world.

When, at the beginning of 1853, the foes of the Bábí movement considered their work, they thought their purpose fully accomplished, their victory complete. The Báb was dead. His name was anathema. If any of his votaries survived, they were cowed and silent. No sign or trace of that brief impetuous crusade which had almost shaken a dead land to life was now anywhere visible save perhaps some bloodstains on the stones of a dismantled fort or the poor fragments of some burned and mutilated body still hanging by a city gate to remind the beholder of the awful malediction laid on that proscribed and execrated faith.

CHAPTER VII

THE ENTRANCE OF THE KING OF GLORY

In this determined and ruthless campaign against the Bábí Faith the Persian government made, however, two mistakes of so serious a nature as to render nugatory all their scheming and cruelty and to transform an apparent success into complete failure. In the first place, they forgot the adage that the blood of the martyrs is the seed of the Church, and they could not conceive that their efforts to suppress the truth by physical violence were driving it to seek a hiding-place deeper in the hearts of the people. This blunder is after more than a hundred years obvious to all observers, but it began to be evident even while the life-blood of the Bábís was being poured forth upon the earth. Professor Browne states in his *A Year Amongst the Persians*:

> The barbarity of the persecutors defeated its own ends, and, instead of inspiring terror, gave the martyrs an opportunity of exhibiting a heroic fortitude which has done more than any propaganda, however skilful, could have done to ensure the triumph of the cause for which they died . . . The impression produced by such exhibitions of courage and endurance was profound and lasting; nay, the faith which inspired the martyrs was often contagious, as the following incident shows. A certain Yezdí rough, noted for his wild and disorderly life, went to see the execution of some Bábís, perhaps to scoff at them. But when he saw with what calmness and steadfastness they met torture and death, his feelings underwent so great a revulsion that he

rushed forward crying, 'Kill me too! I also am a Bábí!'
And thus he continued to cry till he too was made a
partaker in the doom he had come out only to gaze
upon.[1]

Today the record of those immortal martyrs still stirs
the blood and quickens the faith of those who read it.
The infamy of the persecutions has long since helped to
carry the story far and wide, and has awakened in distant
lands sympathy with the sufferers and admiration for that
youthful 'Charmer of Hearts' (as they called him), for
whom men, women and children counted it happiness
to face torture and death. Outwardly among the peoples,
inwardly in men's souls, the efforts of the enemies of
God were turned against themselves and became the
means of propagating the new gospel and of fixing it on
spiritual foundations from which it can never be removed.

To this mistake the Persian Government added another
more signal. They had destroyed every Bábí who had
shown any capacity for leadership except one.

They had not fully realised that of all the champions of
the New Revelation the most powerful was Bahá'u'lláh.
His eminent social position and his outstanding reputation as a man and as a citizen had, to some degree, protected him; while his acumen and prudence had enabled
him to combine the greatest possible amount of activity
with the least possible amount of provocation. After the
attempt on the Sháh's life, he was seized and without
trial thrust into a dungeon in Ṭihrán. The chamber in
which he was confined was buried deep underground and
received no light nor air save what could pass down three
steep flights of narrow stairs. Weighted with heavy chains
which bent his back and galled his neck, having a number
of the basest criminals of the empire for his companions,
and being kept in daily expectation of his execution, he

was held here for four months, under conditions too revolting to bear description. In the end, his innocence being established, and the authorities being informed that his health was now so broken that he certainly must soon die, he was taken up out of the prison, degraded and despoiled, and sent with his family into perpetual exile.

In issuing this sentence of banishment, and in afterwards directing his course through Constantinople and Adrianople to the Holy Land, his enemies forgot that their Prophet Muḥammad had many times and with a strange emphasis called the attention of the faithful to the City of 'Akká. He had said:

'Akká is a city in Syria to which God hath shown His special mercy.

And again:

Of all shores the best is the shore of Askelon, and 'Akká is, verily, better than Askelon, and the merit of 'Akká above that of Askelon and all other shores is as the merit of Muḥammad above that of all other Prophets. I bring you tidings of a city betwixt two mountains in Syria, in the middle of a meadow, which is called 'Akká. Verily, he that entereth therein, longing for it and eager to visit it, God will forgive his sins, both of the past and of the future.

And again:

By the shore of the sea is a city, suspended beneath the Throne, and named 'Akká. He that dwelleth therein, firm and expecting a reward from God—exalted be He—God will write down for him, until the Day of Resurrection, the recompense of such as have

been patient, and have stood up, and knelt down, and
prostrated themselves, before Him.

And again:

> I announce unto you a city, on the shores of the sea,
> white, whose whiteness is pleasing unto God—exalted
> be He! It is called 'Akká . . . And he that raiseth
> therein the call to prayer, his voice will be lifted up unto
> Paradise . . . There are kings and princes in Paradise.
> The poor of 'Akká are the kings of Paradise and the
> princes thereof. A month in 'Akká is better than a
> thousand years elsewhere . . . Blessed the man that
> hath visited 'Akká, and blessed he that hath visited the
> visitor of 'Akká.[2]

Finally, to Muḥammad is attributed the statement that
'all of them [meaning the companions of the Qá'im] shall
be slain except One who shall reach the plain of 'Akká,
the Banquet-Hall of God'.[3]

The government's slaughter of the Báb and all his abler
companions save only one, and its sentence upon that one
of banishment to the gaol-city of 'Akká, were thus preg-
nant with ironic significance; and while seeming to spell
ignominy and destruction, in reality drew upon the Báb
and Bahá'u'lláh the light and glory of divine prediction.

From childhood, and indeed from birth, subtle intima-
tions and open portents had marked out Mírzá Ḥusayn-
'Alí, eldest son of the Vizir Mírzá Buzurg, as him whom
God should manifest. When he was born on November
12th, 1817, at the hour of dawn in Ṭíhrán, a disciple of
Aḥmad-i-Aḥsá'í (the forerunner of the Báb) who was then
resident in Náyin, bowing to the ground in an access of
wonder, testified that 'at this very hour the light of the
promised One has broken and is shedding illumination
upon the world'.[4]

His father had marked him as a child of extraordinary promise, and his opinion was confirmed by a strange dream in which he saw his son swimming in a boundless sea, his body shining like the sun and his black hair floating across the waters. The fishes gathered about him, and each seized and held the end of one of his hairs as he swam; but not a hair was dislodged from his head, nor was his movement through the waters impeded. A famous soothsayer, being brought in to interpret this dream, explained that the sea was the world of being, the fishes were the peoples of the earth who would gather about Bahá'u'lláh and cling to him, that the disturbance of their movement through the waters was the turmoil Bahá'u'lláh would cause among men, and that as no hair was broken nor drawn from his head, so should his person, though he should be quite alone, remain safe through all dangers.

Some years later an eminent jurist, Mujtahid Mírzá Muḥammad Taqíy-i-Núrí, having occasion in the course of his lectures on the law of Islám to speak of Bahá'u'lláh, then a young man of twenty-four or twenty-five years of age, told his listeners he had had two dreams lately in which Bahá'u'lláh had figured and that he thought them of high significance. In one he dreamed that he made his way through a concourse of people to a house in which, they said, the promised Qá'im dwelt; but his eager efforts to enter were refused because, within, the Qá'im was engaged in a private colloquy and could not be disturbed. He with whom the prophet thus confidently talked proved to be none other than Bahá'u'lláh. In the other dream, the Mujtahid seemed to be in a library in which he saw a number of books that belonged to Bahá'u'lláh, and were stored in coffers. Opening these books, he found that every word and every letter inscribed therein was illumined with the most exquisite jewels.

Bahá'u'lláh was of a deeply religious nature and from his early boyhood determined to devote his life to the cause of religion. This choice was a departure from the tradition of his family which pointed him to the service of the State rather than to that of the Church. His forefathers had played a leading part in the administration of the country and had held high ministerial offices under the Crown. His father himself was a distinguished Vizir, and the young heir was expected by all to follow in the footsteps of his ancestors. When his friends observed in him the rapid development of great powers and perceived the keenness of his intelligence, the vigour of his will, his charm of manner and eloquence of tongue, they predicted that his success would be outstanding and that his career would add lustre to the noble record of a family of able administrators. When the young man showed no inclination to enter the sphere of politics, their surprise was great; but they trusted his judgment, assuring themselves that 'he knows what he is doing; he has his own purpose'.

In devoting himself to the cause of religion, Bahá-'u'lláh did not become an ecclesiastic nor study in a theological school. He was brought up as a layman, and wore that lambskin hat or kuláh which was in Persia the badge of those who follow a secular rather than a clerical calling. He frequently took part, publicly as well as in private, in discussions on spiritual matters and on the spiritual aspects of Islámic law, and gained a great reputation for his insight and understanding. 'His speech,' writes Dr. T. K. Cheyne, 'was like a rushing torrent, and his clearness in exposition brought the most learned divines to his feet.' But he was without learning or academic training, and his knowledge was attested by all as that of a genius, not of a scholar.

The first overt act by which Bahá'u'lláh exposed the

inner purpose of his life was his espousal of the cause of the Báb. As soon as he heard of the Báb's appearance he proclaimed himself a Bábí, and throwing himself heart and soul into the movement he did all that insight and enthusiasm could do to lay the foundations of the faith deep in the hearts of his countrymen.

Three years after the Báb's martyrdom, at a time when the Cause seemed to be at its lowest ebb, Bahá'u'lláh alluded in some of his odes to his station as the Central Figure of the whole movement which the Báb had initiated.

The Báb had anticipated this declaration, specifying its date ('the year nine', he had said, meaning the ninth year of his own dispensation), and had not only implied by several signs the identity of Bahá'u'lláh as the Promised One of all ages, but had explicitly shown it to one or two of his own most trusted apostles.

By this intimation Bahá'u'lláh unburdened his heart of the divine secret committed to him and made clear the motive which had led him to depart from his family tradition and choose instead the religious life. But the reference was of a private and preparatory nature. The Báb's Era continued: the Báb's writ still ran. The time had not yet fully come for Bahá'u'lláh's formal proclamation of his prophethood and for his assumption of direct sovereignty.

The proclamation was an event of the deepest moment and fraught with far-reaching and immeasurable consequences. In the first place the Prophet's pronouncement of a New Era would bring the former Era to an end and would abstract from its ordinances, customs, rites and institutions their authority and influence. The Era of the Báb bore indeed to that which followed it a special and unparalleled relation. The Báb had the station of an independent High-Prophet, directly informed by the Most

High. But his function was that of Bahá'u'lláh's immediate forerunner. His Era was very short, the shortest known to human records, extending over only nineteen years. So closely was his work connected with that of his Supreme Lord that the year of the Báb's Declaration is continued as the date of the New Era. Bahá'u'lláh has ordained 1844 as the beginning of the Dispensation of the Glory of God. Yet the Declaration of Bahá'u'lláh would mark the birthday of a new system, a new economy, a new morality, a new obligation and a new loyalty. It would also introduce into that psychological realm, where mankind's thoughts and feelings have their source, the impact of a fresh spiritual influence and generative force. In matters of nearer and more direct concern the High-Prophet's open assumption of his office would set him in a new relation to the men of his own time, whether they recognised him or not, showing up weakness and error, however closely veiled, and covering with glory the true-hearted and the faithful. Moreover, it would involve the Prophet personally in a number of new responsibilities and difficulties which would call for the exercise of the most delicate tact and judgment, would heighten the hostility and opposition of many, and would bring upon him fresh suffering and trial.

Ten years passed before Bahá'u'lláh, in the spring of 1863, decided that the moment was come for his explicit Declaration. His long sojourn in Baghdád was closing. The misrepresentations of an enemy had intensified the suspicions of the authorities, and he was under sentence of removal to a more distant place of exile, where he was to be held in stricter ward. His personal position was full of danger, and the future was laden with the darkest threats. But to be weighed down with care or discouraged by calamities was not the way of Bahá'u'lláh. His self-

annunciation, however unworthy the earthly circumstances amidst which it was made, was in reality an
occasion of triumph and rejoicing. It notified to mankind
that God's promised blessings were no longer in the
future but were now at hand, that the Ancient Covenant
was completed, that Doomsday, the Day of the Lord,
had broken upon the world, and that he who had been
so long heralded as the Everlasting Father was about to
bring to his children the realisation of their brotherhood
and to dwell on earth among them. In spite of his personal
embarrassments Bahá'u'lláh invested his Declaration with
dignity and impressiveness, making it a unique season of
holy festival in which the social happiness of believers
mirrored the joy that was among the angels in heaven.
The spot which he chose for the event was a garden
outside the town of Baghdád where he and his family had
withdrawn while the caravan was being made ready for
the long journey to Constantinople. While in the garden,
April 21st to May 2nd, 1863, he made his Declaration.
So powerful was the radiance of his spirit that the despair
of these followers who were now to be separated from
their beloved Lord and friend was transmuted by his
influence. They dried their tears, put away their sorrow
and grasping through his inspiration the profound
significance of the moment they partook of his spiritual
enthusiasm and were transported with a joy breathed on
them from heaven.

During his sojourn in Baghdád Bahá'u'lláh had won
the warm affection and admiration of all classes; his
friends were legion. Now at his departure crowds of
people high and low, rich and poor, from the governor
and the nobility to those of low degree, streamed out to
his retreat to bid him a reluctant farewell. The greatness
of the concourse that thronged about him day after day,
the sympathy and sense of irreparable loss which all ex-

pressed, the radiant devotion of his followers whose
spiritual illumination had driven away unhappiness, constituted a spontaneous public tribute to the charm and
power of his personality and afforded a not unsuitable
setting to the mystical event of a High-Prophet's
Declaration.

In that solemn pronouncement Bahá'u'lláh at last gave
full expression to the resolution which he had formed in
childhood, and which in the face of gathering difficulties
he was to pursue to his life's end. He made his statement
openly in the presence of a number of chosen believers,
but he did not blazon nor press it upon the notice of the
public. He had put the truth within their reach, and it was
their responsibility to take the knowledge which he had
offered them. Among the faithful a great change gradually took shape. Bahá'u'lláh was venerated no longer
simply as the chieftain of the Bábís. His authority now
was independent. His broader teachings supplanted the
preparatory teaching of his forerunner. The name Bábí
by degrees gave way to the name Bahá'í. But the attitude
of non-believers remained as before. Few indeed knew of
his pronouncement, none understood it. The envy and
malignity of his private enemies probably was intensified;
certainly they continued to outjudas Judas. And the
governments of the Sháh and the Sultán continued to
pursue a policy of condemnation and repression.

Nineteen years before, when he had first espoused the
cause of the Báb, Bahá'u'lláh was in his golden youth endowed with all that fills life with pleasantness and hope:
rank, wealth, health, popularity and growing fame. Now
when he assumed the full responsibilities of his divinely-
given office he had been denuded of all that could be
taken from him. He was homeless, destitute, branded, a
captive, an exile, with the threat of further punishment
held over his head. Only his life (according to the strange

predictive dream of his boyhood) had been preserved by God from the powers of his enemies. Despoiled of all those facilities for propagating the cause which originally he had had in so great a measure, and left with nothing on earth but those inalienable gifts of mind and heart which he had from his Maker alone, Bahá'u'lláh was at the same time the victim of active restraints and positive afflictions. He underwent at the hands of the government every variety of punishment: now he suffered from cruel exposure, now from continued and close confinement; now he was subjected to torture, now weakened by long privation. More than once the inhumanities inflicted on him brought him to the verge of death, and a hundred times his life was in peril from the anger of a despotic master or the rage of a howling mob. He was compelled from the time of his exile onward to the end of his life to watch those most near and dear to him endure for love of him calamities only less than his own, and to see them in many instances untimely sink and die under their miseries. Not until his closing days was there any abatement of the rigours of his captivity, and he died as he had lived, a prisoner and an exile, far from that fair and well-loved land in which he and his forefathers had reigned in ducal affluence and splendour.

In spite of all his difficulties Bahá'u'lláh pursued with inflexible determination the path which he from the beginning had marked out for himself. No obstacle stopped his progress; no discouragement lowered his enthusiasm; adversity did not break nor wretchedness weaken his equanimity and confidence. His will was adamant. His spiritual powers inexhaustible.

Throughout his career his attitude towards this persecution and towards those responsible for it was marked by an extraordinary independence. He was acutely conscious of its injustice and constantly protested against his wrongs in the most vigorous language. In one of his earliest works, *The Hidden Words*, he referred to himself and to the treatment meted out to him thus:

O Dwellers of the city of love! Mortal blasts have beset the everlasting candle, and the beauty of the celestial Youth is veiled in the darkness of dust. The chief of the monarchs of love is wronged by the people of tyranny and the dove of holiness lies prisoned in the talons of owls. The dwellers in the pavilion of glory and the celestial concourse bewail and lament, while ye repose in the realms of negligence, and esteem yourselves as of the true friends. How vain are your imaginings![5]

He constantly referred to himself as 'This Oppressed One', and in his epistles set forth his wrongs. Writing to Napoleon III he said:

He, for Whose sake the world was called into being, hath been imprisoned in the most desolate of cities ('Akká), by reason of that which the hands of the wayward have wrought. From the horizon of His prison-city He summoneth mankind unto the Dayspring of God, the Exalted, the Great.[6]

To the Czar of Russia he wrote, 'Know thou that though My body be beneath the swords of My foes, and My limbs be beset with incalculable afflictions, yet My spirit is filled with a gladness with which all the joys of the earth can never compare.'[7] Towards the end of his life, in 1890, he wrote in his *Epistle to the Son of the Wolf*:

. . . they have incited a great many . . . and are busying themselves in spreading calumnies. It is clear and

evident that they will surround with their swords of
hatred and their shafts of enmity the one whom they
knew to be an outcast among men and to have been
banished from one country to another . . . This
Wronged One, however, remained calm and silent in
the Most Great Prison.[8]

To the Sháh he wrote:

I have seen, O Sháh, in the path of God what eye
hath not seen nor ear heard . . . How numerous the
tribulations which have rained, and will soon rain,
upon Me! I advance with My face set towards Him
Who is the Almighty, the All-Bounteous, whilst behind Me glideth the serpent. Mine eyes have rained
down tears until My bed is drenched. I sorrow not for
Myself, however. By God! Mine head yearneth for the
spear out of love for its Lord. I never passed a tree, but
Mine heart addressed it saying: 'O would that thou
wert cut down in My name, and My body crucified
upon thee, in the path of My Lord!' yea, because I see
mankind going astray in their intoxication, and they
know it not . . . [The rulers] . . . are about to send us
forth from this land [Adrianople], unto the city of
Acre. And, according to what they say, it is assuredly
the most desolate [of cities], . . . the most detestable in
climate, and the foulest in water; it is as though it
were the metropolis of the owl; there is not heard from
its regions aught save the sound of its hooting. And in it
they intend to imprison the servant, and to shut in our
faces the doors of leniency and take away from us the
good things of the life of the world during what re-
maineth of our days.[9]

Even while he painted in such dolorous colours the
afflictions heaped upon him, and with such energy pro-

tested against their injustice, yet Bahá'u'lláh endured
them all with a superhuman patience. 'His strength was
infinite,' said the chief of his intimates. 'You would have
thought he was living in the greatest comfort.' He
affirmed his independence of all his troubles and his
ability to bear undismayed whatever cruelties should be
inflicted on him.

'My calamity is My Providence,' he testifies in *The
Hidden Words*; 'outwardly it is fire and vengeance, but
inwardly it is light and mercy.'[10]

Condemned to imprisonment in 'Akká, he exclaimed:

> . . . Though weariness lay Me low, and hunger con-
> sume Me, and the bare rock be My bed, and My fellows
> the beasts of the field, I will not complain, but will en-
> dure patiently as those endued with constancy and
> firmness have endured patiently, through the power of
> God, the Eternal King and Creator of the nations, and
> will render thanks unto God under all conditions.[11]

In his *Epistle to the Son of the Wolf* he writes:

> . . . it is no secret that I have been, most of the days
> of My life, even as a slave, sitting under a sword hang-
> ing on a thread, knowing not whether it would fall
> soon or late upon him. And yet, notwithstanding all
> this We render thanks unto God, the Lord of the
> worlds. Mine inner tongue reciteth, in the day-time
> and in the night-season, this prayer: 'Glory to Thee, O
> my God! But for the tribulations which are sustained
> in Thy path, how could Thy true lovers be recog-
> nized; . . .'[12]

He bore no resentment against those who maltreated
him, but asked God

... by the sun of Thy grace, and the sea of Thy knowledge, and the heaven of Thy justice, to aid them that have denied Thee to confess, and such as have turned aside from Thee to return, and those who have calumniated Thee to be just and fair-minded.[13]

So complete was the plenitude of his selflessness that he rejoiced in his adversity in so far as it might be made a gain to the faithful. He prayed God 'to make this dark calamity a buckler for the body of his saints, and to protect them thereby from sharp swords and piercing blades'.

'Through affliction,' he added, 'hath His light shone and His praise been bright unceasingly: this has been His method through past ages and bygone times.'[14] No difficulties would stay his course or interrupt him in the execution of his Mission.

Should they hide Me away in the depths of the earth, yet would they find Me riding aloft on the clouds, and calling out unto God, the Lord of strength and of might.[15]

Regarding his persecution from this detached and impersonal point of view he declined to take refuge in flight, even when the door was opened to him, and steadfastly refused to ask the authorities for any favour or to make any entreaty to them on his own behalf. In Constantinople, for example, he was advised by certain friendly noblemen to follow the usual custom and appeal for equity to the Sháh. He gave the remarkable and surely unique reply:

Pursuing the path of obedience to the King's command we have come to this country. Beyond this we neither had nor have any aim or desire that we should appeal and cause trouble. What is [now] hidden behind the veil of destiny will in the future become manifest. There neither has been nor is any necessity for supplication and importunity. If the enlightened-minded leaders [of your nation] be wise and diligent, they will certainly make enquiry, and acquaint themselves with the true state of the case; if not, then [their] attainment of the truth is impracticable and impossible. Under these circumstances what need is there for importuning statesmen and supplicating ministers of the Court? We are free from every anxiety, and . . . prepared for the things predestined to us.[16]

In which statement Bahá'u'lláh implies that while the authorities in appearance are passing judgment upon him, in reality their judgment is passing sentence upon them.

No conditions of life could well have been more unfavourable for the prosecution of a great public mission, or for the production of a vast body of practical and metaphysical instruction. Yet there was one thing granted to Bahá'u'lláh and to 'Abdu'l-Bahá after him which had been denied to the Báb. However dire his sufferings, he was permitted by God's providence to live beyond man's span of seventy years, and when he died in May, 1892, his eye was still undimmed and his natural force unabated. The Báb, owing to the shortness of his life, had not been able to train his followers in the moral precepts of his religion. But Bahá'u'lláh throughout the whole of his active career, found opportunities of teaching by word of mouth and by writing, as well as by example. At first he disseminated among the Bábís the principles set forth by their Lord; afterwards by measured degrees he broadened these into the more universal principles of his own revelation, for which the Báb had opened the way.

During his exile, whether it was in Baghdád, in Constantinople, or Adrianople, he attracted the notice and the admiration of many, and his cause spread widely. Up to the time of his incarceration in 'Akká he made himself generally accessible, mixing with some freedom in society and welcoming visits from inquirers of all kinds. Thoughtful and earnest people of all classes, and indeed of many lands, sought his acquaintance. If distance forbade a personal interview they would communicate with him by letter. He discussed questions of art and science, but more especially problems of religion. So satisfying, so enlightening were his expositions that he created no little stir among the people, and in Adrianople became the centre of a considerable movement. Here it was that his public self-annunciation as God's prophet first began to impress the public; and here it was that the title Bahá'í began to supersede the earlier and preparatory title of Bábí. The success of his teaching in this city was so conspicuous that it inflamed still further the jealousy of his private enemies and instigated that campaign of calumny which involved them as well as himself in yet another sentence of exile. Reaching 'Akká, Bahá'u'lláh at first from necessity and later from choice withdrew into seclusion and devoted himself principally to literary work. The oral instructions given to all and sundry by Bahá'u'lláh during his long pilgrimage from Ṭihrán to 'Akká, and his personal training of those about him, fill a vital place in his mission and have enduring results. But the religion of the Bahá'ís is the religion of a Book. Final authority rests only on the written word of Bahá'u'lláh and of 'Abdu'l-Bahá, duly authenticated. The sole authoritative interpreter of the meaning of these sacred texts is the Guardian, whose pronouncement on the matter is binding on all, even on future Guardians. Texts attributed without verification to Bahá'u'lláh or 'Abdu'l-Bahá or accounts of their lives and their teachings whether they be written by those who knew or heard them, or by others, are to be judged according to their merits: they are not 'gospel'.

The Bahá'ís honour the Scriptures of all preceding religions, including the *Bayán* or works of the Báb, as their Old Testament. Their New Testament consists of the attested writings of Bahá'u'lláh. These are voluminous, and are said to surpass in bulk the whole body of earlier Scriptures. In form they are various, and comprise poems, epigrams, prayers, exhortations, expositions, counsels, laws. Much appears in the form of letters, of some of which Bahá'u'lláh would have a copy made and filed before the despatch of the original. He is said to have composed at great speed, without premeditation and without revision. It was his custom not to write with his own hand but to dictate to secretaries, sometimes continuing with hardly a pause for hours at a time. The style, as a rule, corresponds to this method of composition: its movement is that of a cataract, while the richness of language and imagery and the constant vigour of thought testify to an energy which delights in working at the highest pressure. On the other hand, he would often condense much thought into a little phrase, and would even compose a whole essay or a small book in aphorisms. He wrote in Persian and in Arabic, and is said to have been a master of his medium and to have used the purest diction. Few translations have been made as yet, and out of a total number of compositions which surmise has estimated as one thousand no more than perhaps fifty are now within reach of the English reader: twenty or thirty epistles of varying length, a poem, a parable, some collections of prayers and of precepts.* But however few they be, they are quite sufficient to indicate the character

* The range of translations available in English has increased considerably since the author wrote these words. (Ed.)

E

and the fundamental teachings of the author's religious philosophy. The best known is undoubtedly *The Hidden Words*. This little book of doctrines and precepts was written in Baghdád, and its title, by its reference to a certain Muḥammadan tradition, implies a claim to divine Prophethood. Love and spirituality form its keynote, and its purpose is the religious training of the righteous, 'that they may stand faithful unto the Covenant of God, may fulfil in their lives His trust, and in the realm of spirit obtain the gem of Divine virtue'.[17] It gives sententiously the pith of the prophetic teachings of the past. Justice is the great principle of human life; love is the cause and the end of creation. Man's reunion with God is heaven; separation from God is the source of all misery. God's greatness, his generosity, his forbearance, his displeasure, the menace of his wrath, the promise of man's restoration, all are set forth here.

Akin to this pocket volume are the *Words of Wisdom* which in twenty aphorisms define twenty aspects of spiritual truth.[18] For instance:

The essence of religion is to testify unto that which the Lord hath revealed, and follow that which He hath ordained in His mighty Book.

The source of all glory is acceptance of whatsoever the Lord hath bestowed, and contentment with that which God hath ordained . . .

The source of all learning is the knowledge of God, exalted be His Glory, and this cannot be attained save through the knowledge of His Divine Manifestation.

Bahá'u'lláh's uncompromising monism appears in 'The source of all evil is for man to turn away from his Lord and set his heart on things ungodly'.

Like *The Hidden Words*, the *Book of Certitude* has been

twice rendered into English, the second translation being by the Guardian of the Cause. If *The Hidden Words* be an example of the author's sententiousness, this may stand as an example of his full-flowing eloquence. The argument occupies two hundred and fifty-three pages. It deals with the nature of God's self-revelation to man, and with man's response thereto. It affirms in the first place that those who would gain from a High-Prophet real knowledge of God must make themselves proof against their intellectual, as well as the more material, seductions of earthly existence, and must be freed from prejudice and pride, as well as from a subservient desire for comfort, popularity and the like; and it affirms in the second place that man's attitude to the High-Prophet in his Dispensation must be that of ready, exact and complete obedience, inasmuch as the Prophet is invested by God with the plenitude of divine power and sovereignty. Bahá'u'lláh states his thesis with the utmost vigour and emphasis, showing that the facts of history bear witness to the superhuman authority of all God's Messengers, and that if on their appearance all alike are invariably traduced by their contemporaries the reason is from age to age everlastingly the same. By showing the meaning of apocalyptic texts from Christian and Muḥammadan Scripture, and by drawing parallels between the advents of the past and that of the present, he seeks to save his generation from repeating the historic error of their forefathers and failing to recognise till too late 'the time of their visitation'.

These are doctrinal works; the Covenant and Testament of Bahá'u'lláh is likewise of profound importance to the Bahá'í community and deals with more practical matters.* Bahá'u'lláh here appoints his eldest son, known as 'Abdu'l-Bahá, his successor, making him 'the Centre of the Covenant'—'Whoso turneth towards Him

* *Kitáb-i-'Ahd—The Book of the Covenant.* (Ed.)

hath turned towards God, and whoso turneth away from Him hath turned away from My Beauty, hath repudiated My Proof, and transgressed against Me'[19]—bequeaths certain directions to the people of the world and announces that after himself no High-Prophet will arise for a full thousand years.

Better known to the general reader than these or any other of the writings of Bahá'u'lláh are the letters he addressed to the rulers of the Middle East and of the West, including the *Epistles to the Kings* which were described and analysed by Baron Rosen in the *Bulletin de l'Institut Oriental de Saint-Pétersbourg* and by Professor E. G. Browne in the *Journal of the Royal Asiatic Society*.[*] He wrote to the Sháh, to the Sultán and to his prime minister, to Queen Victoria, to Napoleon III (twice), to the Czar of Russia, to the Pope, and included in the Aqdas [†] messages to the Emperors of Germany and of Austria, and to the Presidents of the American Republics. In these letters he stated that he was suffering a grievous captivity; but his mode of address, though courteous, was not that of a subject to a sovereign, nor of weakness approaching power and grandeur. The style is ringing and the rolling periods are overcharged with the energy of the writer's will. The monarchs are asked to co-operate with the writer in his efforts for the amelioration of the condition of the people, and to promote among their citizens his ideas of fraternity and universal peace through which alone the happiness and prosperity of mankind would be assured. They stand as representatives of God on earth since in them the divine attributes of power and authority are centred, and it is therefore incumbent on them to show forth the attendant qualities of God, such

[*] See *The Proclamation of Bahá'u'lláh* (Bahá'í World Centre, 1967), which gives selected passages from these letters (Tablets). (Ed.)

[†] *Kitáb-i-Aqdas*. (Ed.)

as justice and providence, and to take the greatest care of those committed to their charge. Bahá'u'lláh calls on them to accept and acknowledge the High-Prophet whom God has sent forth for the guidance of mankind, and asseverates that honour and prosperity will bless their reigns through this submission alone.

In these letters Bahá'u'lláh incorporated certain predictions of impending historical events, to which circumstances have drawn some public attention. Other writings also of the Prophet contain predictions, from his *Hidden Words* composed in 1857–8* to the works of his closing years. Some of these predictions are warnings of retribution, of downfall, of defeat, of immense calamity; others are blessings and promises of reward. Some are material in their scope, others spiritual. Some indicate an early fulfilment, others look farther into the future. All are to be realised within a measurable time—not later, it appears, than the end of this century. The most daring, the most dramatic, the most stupendous of all his prophecies are undoubtedly those which lie at the centre of his divine message: his categorical and reiterated assurances that after a period of world-wide purgation human nature is to be regenerated, the nations federated and permanent peace to be established. But the attention of scholars and the public hitherto has been mostly confined to statements which clearly foretold approaching national changes, and which came exactly true according to his word. Thus, writing in 1869 to Napoleon III, then at the zenith of his fortune, Bahá'u'lláh foretold the Emperor's speedy downfall: which occurred the following year. To the chief minister of the Sultán of Turkey he wrote in 1868 from his prison in 'Akká that 'Soon will he seize you in His wrathful anger, and sedition will be stirred up in your midst, and your dominions will be disrupted. Then will

* A.H. 1274. (Ed.)

ye bewail and lament, and will find none to help or succour you . . .'[20] And he foretold an early fall from power, the loss to the Sultán of Adrianople and other places and a general political disruption. On the other hand, to Queen Victoria he promised a long and happy reign. Writing in the early seventies, he issued to Germany (then flushed with victory over the French) a warning of a bloody defeat on her western border, and of yet a second trouble that should thereafter ensue. At the same time he bade Persia:

> Let nothing grieve thee, O Land of Ṭá [Ṭihrán], for God hath chosen thee to be the source of the joy of all mankind. He shall, if it be His will, bless thy throne with one who will rule with justice, who will gather together the flock of God which the wolves have scattered.[21]

Among all his uncounted works, Bahá'u'lláh assigned the first place in importance to the treatise which he named *Kitáb-i-Aqdas*, The Most Holy Book. This has not yet been published in English, but has long been available in the original.* It contains the statutes and the judgments which are to be the law of the Kingdom of God during the New Era. These ordinances are designed to meet the needs of every land and to ensure the continual progress of every people. They are universal in their scope, preserve the liberties of the nations, and are to lead to the harmonisation of all interests and the establishment of enduring concord among the classes and the peoples of the world.

The career of Bahá'u'lláh now has passed into history.

---

* The Universal House of Justice has in hand the publication of a synopsis of the *Kitáb-i-Aqdas* and a codification of the laws and ordinances contained in it. (Ed.)

Nothing can be added to it and nothing taken from it. It stands complete. Those who opposed him have perished, and the system that gave them their opportunity against him has perished with them. The ecclesiastical hierarchy of Persia and of Turkey has been discredited and reduced by its own votaries. The Sultanate and the Caliphate, those ancient institutions of Sunní Islám have been destroyed. But the name and the word of Bahá'u'lláh endure. The record of his life remains to prove what heights of constancy and achievement can in the face of every difficulty be attained by one who has consecrated his will wholly to the omnipotent will of God. His counsels and teachings have spread around the entire globe and brought with them to many comfort, courage and hope. His prescience and his modernity grow ever more evident as the world-changes he forecast take shape in fact and the ideals he promulgated permeate the West and the East, and are hailed as the distinctive marks of our progressive age. His wisdom impresses ever more deeply its claim on men's admiration as the repeated failure of all superficial schemes drives them back upon the truth that the social order of the world will never now be rebuilt till men subject their personal wills to him who is the Source of all unity and the Cause of all concord.

NOTE

Cardinal Dates of the Bahá'í Faith*

1753—1826.	Shaykh Aḥmad of Aḥsá, Arabia: first forerunner of the Báb.
1793—1843.	Siyyid Káẓim: second forerunner of the Báb.
1817, Nov. 12th.	Birth of Bahá'u'lláh.
1819, Oct. 20th.	Birth of the Báb.
1841.	Marriage of the Báb.
1844, May 22nd.	Declaration of the Báb to Mullá Ḥusayn in Shíráz.
1845.	Persecution of the Bábís begins.
1848, July.	Báb's examination in Tabríz.
1849, February.	Death of Mullá Ḥusayn, 'the Gate of the Gate'.
1849, May 16th.	Death of Quddús.
1850, June.	Death of Vaḥíd.
1850, March.	Death of the Seven Martyrs of Ṭihrán.
1850, July 9th.	Death of the Báb.
1851, January.	Death of Ḥujjat.
1852, Aug. 15th.	Attempt on the life of the Sháh.
1852, August.	Death of Ṭáhirih.
	Imprisonment of Bahá'u'lláh.
1853, Jan. 12th.	Banishment of Bahá'u'lláh.
1853, April 8th.	Bahá'u'lláh reaches Baghdád.
1854, April 10th.	Withdraws to wilderness.
1856, March 19th.	Returns from wilderness.

* See *Bahá'í World*, vol. XIII, pp. 756–58, for a more complete list, to April 1963. (Ed.)

1857–62.	Composition of *Seven Valleys, Hidden Words,* and *Kitáb-i-Íqán,* or *Book of Certitude.*
1863, April 22nd.	Declaration of the Mission of Bahá-'u'lláh.
1863, May 3rd.	Departure from Baghdád.
1863, Aug. 16th.	Reaches Constantinople.
1863, Dec. 12th.	Reaches Adrianople.
1863–8.	Composition of *Epistles of the Kings, First Epistle to Napoleon III, Epistle to Sháh of Persia.*
1868, Aug. 31st.	Reaches 'Akká.
1868–91.	Composition of *2nd Epistle to Napoleon, Epistles to Queen Victoria, to the Czar, to the Pope, Epistle to Son of the Wolf.*
1892, May 29th.	Passing of Bahá'u'lláh.
1908, September.	'Abdu'l-Bahá's release from prison.
1910.	'Abdu'l-Bahá in Egypt.
1911.	First Missionary Journey of 'Abdu'l-Bahá (to Geneva, London, Paris).
1912—13.	Second Missionary Journey of 'Abdu'l-Bahá (to U.S.A. and Canada, 1912; to five cities in the British Isles—London, Oxford, Edinburgh, Bristol and Liverpool; to Paris, Stuttgart, Budapest and Vienna).
1920, April 27th.	Knighting of 'Abdu'l-Bahá.
1921, Nov. 28th.	Passing of 'Abdu'l-Bahá.

CHAPTER VIII

THE LIGHT OF THE KING'S LAW

Having proclaimed the Day of God, laid the foundations of his Kingdom in the consciousness of mankind and set forth its principles and laws, Bahá'u'lláh, in the year 1892, at the age of seventy-five years, ascended to the higher world. In a written testament he appointed his eldest son, 'Abdu'l-Bahá, the Interpreter of his Word and the Centre of his Covenant. To him, as to the Great Messenger himself, all believers were now to turn for guidance.

'Abdu'l-Bahá at once took up the task of establishing among men the first beginnings of that new civilisation which his father had planned and ordered. The task was one of the greatest difficulty, even for one who had not spent his life amidst the rigours of a Turkish prison. Nothing but a supreme and loving trust in Bahá'u'lláh could have supported a man of sober judgment in attempting to build an earthly Paradise in such a world as this.

We are too near in time to Bahá'u'lláh, too enfeebled by the mental habits of an unregenerate past, to be able to grasp the meaning of his constructive work, or to form a picture of the new society that is to arise under his command. But 'Abdu'l-Bahá, out of his father's Revelation, has set forth the main features of the divine scheme, and has explained in clear perspective the central truths and instructions round which humanity is to be reordered and reorganised.

The Lord Christ on that day when his disciples came to him and said, 'Lord, teach us to pray, as John also taught his disciples,' must surely have looked far into the eternal realm and have seen there the spiritual likeness of the world of Bahá'u'lláh. For that which in this time of the End has been brought down to men is the exact fulfilment of that prayer which Christ taught his disciples, and which Christendom has down the ages repeated after him. 'Our Father which art in heaven, Hallowed be thy name. Thy kingdom come. Thy will be done in earth, as *it is* in heaven.' Through the regenerative and creative might of Bahá'u'lláh the attributes of the Most High are now in very fact to be honoured among men, and their opposites held in hate and scorn. Justice, kindness, compassion, truthfulness, faithfulness and the like, are to reign in the place of those satanic qualities whose dominion has hitherto made human history a tale of sadness and shame. The Kingdom which now has come down upon the earth is not the Kingdom of a High-Prophet, nor is this Dispensation called by any High-Prophet's title: rather this Age is the Age of God Himself, this Kingdom the Kingdom of God manifest in his glory.

With the name of this Day Thou hast adorned Thy Tablet which is known only to Thee. Thou hast called it The Day of God. In it nothing is to be seen save Thy Supreme Self, and nothing is to be heard save Thy sweetest Name. Wherefore when He appeared the nations were shaken to their foundations, the learned were bewildered, the wise confounded, save those who turned to Thee . . .

In this Day it is required by Bahá'u'lláh that the will of God be done by men; and men shall be judged by their deeds and by nothing else. Faith in the past has been shown by words. But it is not so now. 'The essence of faith is fewness of words and abundance of deeds . . .'[1] And again:

Guidance hath ever been given by words, and now it is given by deeds. Every one must show forth deeds that are pure and holy, for words are the property of all alike, whereas such deeds as these belong only to Our loved ones. Strive then with heart and soul to distinguish yourselves by your deeds.[2]

Men under former systems have been accepted on their professions, and have been classed according to their lip-statements of belief. Now by express command of God a man is required to prove himself this or that by his conduct.

Thus have Christ and those who devoutly have repeated this prayer opened the way for the millennial reign of Bahá'u'lláh, and those who are citizens of the New Kingdom, under whatever Confession they were reared, acknowledge with gratitude the aid of that ancient prayer that now has found fulfilment.

For the first, the most eminent, the most vital of the great truths which distinguish this Revelation from all others is this: that God's love has won over the hearts of men, and that his dominion on the earth is complete and permanent. This is not the Age of the Promise renewed but of the Promise kept. It does not bring to man a new phase or a new aspect of the Ancient Covenant, but brings the fulfilment of that Covenant in its completeness. The epigram that man never is but always to be blest has in times gone by been true; but it is true no longer—it is out of date and now is false. Blessedness is at the door. God hitherto has endured the waywardness and rebellion of mankind in its immaturity; his mercy has protected them from the natural penalty of their disobedience. He has suffered the tares to grow among the wheat, the bad to be gathered into the fold with the good, and his sun has shone upon the just and the unjust alike. But his patience now is at an end. The appointed time for the weeding out of the tares, for the rejection of the insincere, for the destruction by fire of all workers of iniquity is come in very deed at last. The vision which in its beauty and its terror closes the Bible is no longer to be unveiled to the eye of a seer alone, but is to stand upon the earth before the eyes of all, embodied in historic fact. The poet's pictures of a Golden Age are to seem no more 'such stuff as dreams are made on', but are to be realised by every living soul as an inspired anticipation of that which this present Age unfolds. A far-reaching metamorphosis of man's outer world and his inner world, of society and of thought, is already taking place; and the power by which this change is enforced is the unchangeable decree of the Most High God.

Bahá'u'lláh leaves no doubt as to the meaning of the victory of God and the triumph of his Cause. It does not mean what in previous Dispensations the followers of a High-Prophet have usually understood the triumph of his Cause to mean. It does not mean factiousness, much less strife.

> The meaning of victory is not this, that anyone should fight or strive with another. . . . That which God— glorious is His mention—has desired for Himself is the hearts of His servants, which are treasures of praise and love of the Lord, and are stores of divine knowledge and wisdom . . . Today victory neither has been, nor will be, opposition to anyone, nor strife with any person; but rather, what is well-pleasing is that the cities of men's hearts, which are under the dominion of the hosts of selfishness and desire, should be subdued by the sword of the word, of wisdom and of exhortation. Everyone then who desires victory must first subdue the city of his own heart with the sword of

spiritual truth and of the Word, and must protect it from remembering aught but God; afterwards let him turn his efforts towards the citadel of the hearts of others. This is what is intended by victory. Sedition has never been, nor will be, pleasing to God, and that which certain ignorant persons formerly wrought was never approved by God. If you are slain for His good pleasure, verily it is better for you than that you should slay.[3]

When God's throne is set up within men's hearts, his writ will run without opposition or question. No land, no people, no activity, will lie beyond its jurisdiction. The arts, the sciences, all the occupations of all sections of society, will be grouped around one centre, and will be pursued by men who share a common devotion and a universal obedience.

Such is the most important of the truths set forth by Bahá'u'lláh and made effective by his Will. On this all else depends, and from this all else proceeds.

The Revelation of Bahá'u'lláh, therefore, does not deal alone with pure religion. It is concerned with more than man's soul-attitude towards God and God's creation. It is a social, as well as a spiritual, gospel. It involves indeed a reorientation of many phases of life, and it offers counsel and direction along many lines of endeavour.

The Bahá'í community is to be a hive of activity and co-operation. Social intercourse and festal gatherings are encouraged. There are no recluses. All share the simple ordinary life of humanity. Marriage is commended and shown as consistent with, indeed, conducive to, the highest spiritual attainment—all the three great examples, Bahá'u'lláh, the Báb and 'Abdu'l-Bahá were married. There are no idlers nor parasites. Every man must have a business or profession of some kind, and work done in the spirit of service to society is accepted by God as an act of worship to himself.

'The best of men are they that earn a livelihood by their calling and spend upon themselves and upon their kindred for the love of God, the Lord of all worlds.' Men and women will all meet upon the level. 'Know ye not why We created you all from the same dust? That no one should exalt himself over the other.'[4] But inequalities will remain. Inequality is found everywhere in creation, from the thistle to the cedar, from the atom to Mount Everest; otherwise there would be no world. Men will always be different in character, in aptitude and in ability. Some will be wiser, or more influential, or nearer to God than others. Some will be more affluent, others poorer: the care of the needy, the distressed, and of orphans is committed to those who are able to help as well as to the authorities.

Nor are all callings of indifferent value. Agriculture is esteemed as of primary importance because on it depends the existence of the people. It is the basis of Bahá'u'lláh's economic system. A high place is given to the arts, particularly to music, and those who practise these are given a place of honour. Constitutional monarchy is approved, though not enjoined, as a form of government, partly because it saves the people from the disorder and the expense entailed by frequent elections of the chief officer of the state, and partly because the king is a symbol of the unity of God. Loyalty to the constituted authorities is incumbent on all Bahá'ís. The highest of all callings is that of the teacher of religion. But in the world of Bahá'u'lláh there are no professional clergy, no ecclesiastical class or caste of any kind. There are no rites, nor is there any room or opportunity for the appearance of priestcraft in any shape or form. Teachers of religion are not paid for their teaching, and must gain their livelihood from some other source. Their merit as teacher depends on their purity of purpose, and their efficacy on their being prompted in their work solely by a desire that God should be known. Auricular confession is prohibited because confession to another man 'does not tend to the forgiveness of God'. The era of Bahá'u'lláh is the era of individual responsibility. On every man is laid expressly the duty of investigating the truth for himself. He is not to be content to play in life at the game of 'Follow your leader'; he is not idly to accept tradition, nor idly take his opinions from other men. Oppression and subservience of any kind are not to be in the Bahá'í world. As Christ foretold that the reign of social injustice would mark the end of his Dispensation, so Bahá'u'lláh has poured forth the thunders of his indignation upon tyrants and all tyranny, and has sworn that God will put an end to it.

O oppressors of earth! Withdraw your hands from tyranny, for I have pledged Myself not to forgive any man's injustice. This is My covenant which I have irrevocably decreed in the preserved tablet and sealed it with My seal of glory.[5]

Justice he sets forth as the great principle in the Law of God: 'The best beloved of all things in My sight is Justice.' On this is based the social order, and on it the individual, too, is to rely for real advance in independence and wisdom.

Turn not away [from justice] if thou desirest Me, and neglect it not that I may confide in thee. By its aid thou shalt see with thine own eyes and not through the eyes of others, and shalt know of thine own knowledge and not through the knowledge of thy neighbour . . . Verily justice is My gift to thee and the sign of My loving-kindness. Set it then before thine eyes.[6]

On the other hand, Bahá'u'lláh warns men strongly against mistaken praise of liberty. It is not a boon save when limited and regulated. On the contrary, it is a cause of chaos and leads to destruction. All goodness depends on the abandonment of a falsely conceived individualistic liberty.

'The source of all good is trust in God, submission unto His command, and contentment with His holy will and pleasure . . .'[7] The Bahá'í is trained to think less about his liberty than about the purpose with which he was given that liberty by his Lord. He looks for his ideal to One who chose as his title, 'The Bond Servant of God', and from that example he learns to seek to use all his faculties to their fullest extent, but never to let self-expression be carried to the length of self-emphasis. 'Blessed is he who prefers others to himself,' said Bahá'u'lláh. The law of justice bids a man choose for others what he chooses for himself; the law of mercy to help others regardless of himself.

The duty of the group, on the other hand, is in the first place to preserve order and harmony, and in the second to give the personalities of the various members the fullest scope in working for the common good. On each and all who belong to the group lies the responsibility of preserving this balance, and God gives his special aid to their sincere endeavours.

The citizen of the Kingdom is expected to have the right mental attitude, not only towards such and such particular groups, but also in like measure towards that all-inclusive group, the human race. 'Let not a man glory in this,' said Bahá'u'lláh to Professor Browne, 'that he loves his country; let him rather glory in this, that he loves his kind . . .'[8]

Bahá'u'lláh suffered and toiled for the whole of humanity.

He did not address his appeal to any section. He did not aim to revive any one religion, nor to reform any special civilisation. His outlook was world-wide; his teaching from beginning to end universal. The distinction of his Revelation from all before it is that by the Ancient Decree of God it is to be accepted by all humanity. There will be no more a number of concurrent systems of faith and order, but one system elaborated and expressed by the agreement of all nations. The consciousness of the human race has now in the fullness of time reached a new degree of development. It is capable of appreciating at last the unity of the race. To this education every one of the High-Prophets of the past has contributed his share. The work of none of them is lost. The work of all lives still in the attainment of the race today. Now through the Supreme Advent of Bahá'u'lláh it is completed by a new and crowning bestowal of the grace of the Everlasting God and of his Holy Spirit. Men everywhere are now to believe and know at last the truth of the old revelation that there is one Father of us all, that the earth is one home, and that all men are brothers, and this belief is to direct conduct and to become the basis of the new world-order. Bahá'u'lláh has bidden all his followers to purge their hearts of all religious and racial prejudices, and of all national or racial animosities. Obedience to this command is held today as the hall-mark of the loyal Bahá'í. Jews, Christians, Parsees, Muslims, Buddhists, Agnostics, Free-thinkers—all met together at the table of 'Abdu'l-Bahá and enjoyed the same consideration and the same privileges. In his presence differences were forgotten; the underlying brotherhood became all in all. What moral effort and breadth of mind unaided would hardly accomplish, would happen in a moment through the inspiration of Bahá'u'lláh.

The unification of mankind is accordingly the first great

practical task which the High-Prophet laid upon his followers. Success in that task is made possible, nay insured,
by the special intervention of God, but it will not come
about of its own accord. Its accomplishment will need
effort. If that effort be not promptly made, unnecessary
delay will cause great and increasing tribulation.

Bahá'u'lláh would—it seems—have brought his message in person to the peoples of the West, but was prevented from doing so by his enemies, who kept him a
prisoner to the day of his death. It fell to the lot of his
son, 'Abdu'l-Bahá, to carry out this project and to travel
across Europe and the United States as far as San Francisco
proclaiming the Cause and explaining the primary principles of Bahá'u'lláh's scheme, for the unification of mankind.

'Abdu'l-Bahá drew attention in the first place to the fact
that God in this Age had removed those geographical
barriers which hitherto had separated nation from nation,
and which had impeded the spread of all past Revelations.
He had taught men improved methods of locomotion and
communication, and had thus in his good time created
those physical conditions which would enable the peoples
of the East and the West to unite their activities and to
form themselves into an organic union.

The removal of traditional misunderstandings and in-
veterate prejudice was another matter. Towards this end
Bahá'u'lláh ordained that all peoples should henceforth
be bilingual and should share one universal tongue, in
addition to having their own separate national tongues.
This universal medium should either be one of the languages already in use or should be a special composite
structure.

Bahá'u'lláh set forth for convenience of world-use a
universal calendar also, to be employed by all peoples,
instead of the rival systems now in use. For this purpose

he adopted, with a slight adjustment, that already created by the Báb. In this, as in the ancient Greek calendar of Meton, familiar to the West through the Golden Numbers, the cardinal number of the system is nineteen. There are nineteen days in each month, and nineteen months in the year, with four or five intercalary days to make the calendar correspond with the solar year, and the years are grouped in cycles of nineteen. The names of the months are taken from attributes of God, such as Splendour, Glory, Beauty, Grandeur, Light, Mercy and the like.

The immense importance attached to education (as well as to learning and culture generally), constitutes one of the outstanding features of the Bahá'í economy and religion. This appears throughout the writings of Bahá'u'lláh in many forms, through some allusion or implication as well as in definite statement or express provision. For instance, in the statute regarding bequests, the principle that a teacher is truly in an intellectual sense a father to his pupil is made the basis of a legal enactment. Or again it is laid down that the schooling of a daughter, as a future mother, takes precedence over that of a son, for the significant reason that in a family the first teacher of the children is the mother and that her responsibility in this regard must be specially looked to from the beginning.

The general care of the diviner and humaner letters throughout the world is entrusted to a College of International Teachers, who are appointed by the Guardian, he himself as the ordained Interpreter of the Sacred Text being Teacher in Chief. This body elects from its own number a special Staff or Chapter of nine members whose special business it is to work in the closest association with the Chief Teacher. The system of education to be pursued among the nations has in its character and broad outlines been defined by Bahá'u'lláh. It will provide for students of all ages and of both sexes, of every grade of intelligence. It will not be confined to the leading races, but will include all, not being complete till peoples now in a primitive condition come within its scope. Its range will be ample and diversified enough to give full play to every variety of taste and talent. No nation will find its special needs and peculiar interests sacrificed to those of any other nation, nor to those of the whole. The particular abilities of all will be encouraged and developed. Indeed, the general purpose of the great educational scheme will be to bring every human power and faculty to its best perfection in order that the race—regarded as a whole—may reach the highest practicable degree of knowledge and efficiency.

On the other hand, the distortion of national history, the perpetuation of local suspicions and animosities, the inculcation of narrow or separatist views will be prevented. The drift and spirit of all the information given to each student will have been approved by an international Board, and all that the student is taught will be in accord with the instruction given to every other student everywhere.

The establishment of these educational principles will be a prerequisite of any real unification of mankind. It will constitute, too, a strong and permanent basis for a single world-culture, a universal civilisation.

To give stability to such a civilisation, and to set a mould in which it will take form and shape, Bahá'u'lláh has included in his teaching certain economic regulations, taken over almost wholly from the writings of the Báb, and also a number of important ordinances in the field of both civil and criminal law. The economic and the legal system are both to run throughout the entire globe. Class distinctions, in the odious sense, will fade out; but there will always be differences in social status, for the reason that members of an army cannot all be privates nor all be generals. Capital will remain, but extremes of wealth and poverty will be prevented, and the hardships caused by the present struggle for existence will be alleviated. No private citizen will carry weapons of offence. Every national government, however, will have its corps of police to preserve order, and the central world-government will have a paramount police force to maintain peace among the nations and to reduce to subjection any aggressor.

At the apex of this administrative system stand two high Responsibilities, two signal Institutions: the Guardianship, and the Universal House of Justice.* The Guardian is the centre and the representative of the unity of the Cause and of the believers. He is denominated by 'Abdu'l-Bahá 'the Sign of God, the Chosen Branch, the Interpreter of the Words of God'. The office is hereditary, and descends normally to the eldest son. But it is to be noted that even in this hereditary office (as in all the other offices of the Bahá'í administration) godliness of character is an essential prerequisite. Each Guardian is in his own lifetime to designate his successor. Should his first-born son not be spiritually worthy of his post, should he not be 'detached from worldly things, the essence of purity'; should he not 'show in himself the fear of God, knowledge, wisdom and understanding', the Guardian is to pass him over and to choose 'another branch' in his stead.

The Guardian has the privilege also of appointing the College of International Teachers, the 'Hands of the Cause', whose function is 'to diffuse the divine fragrances, to edify the souls of men, to promote learning, to improve

* First elected in April, 1963, the electors being members of the National Spiritual Assemblies of the Bahá'í world, who met in a World Convention in Haifa, Israel. (Ed.)

the character of all men and to be at all times and under all conditions sanctified and detached from earthly things'. These Teachers elect from their own number a Council of Nine who are to devote themselves entirely to aiding the Guardian in his work.*

The Universal House of Justice, with the Guardian as its chairman, is the supreme legislative body of the Bahá'í world. To it is reserved the privilege of making statutes and ordinances on all matters not expressly dealt with in the Aqdas, and also of modifying or rescinding its own enactments if occasion arise. Rigidity in the legal system is thus avoided, and sufficient provision made for the adjustment of the law to the changing needs of a continually developing world.

By both Bahá'u'lláh and 'Abdu'l-Bahá order and discipline in the Bahá'í community are vigorously insisted on. The Guardian and the Universal House of Justice are under the particular protection of the All-Wise, and any form of disobedience to them in their respective spheres is forbidden under penalty of the dire wrath of God.

The general scheme of world-administration towards which the Bahá'ís are working is thus outlined by the Guardian of the Cause in an exposition of certain passages contained in the Epistle which Bahá'u'lláh wrote and despatched to Queen Victoria in 1868.

What else could these weighty words signify if they did not point to the inevitable curtailment of unfettered national sovereignty as an indispensable preliminary to the formation of the future Commonwealth of all the nations of the world? Some form of a world Super-State must needs be evolved, in whose favour all the nations of the world will have willingly ceded every

* These nine are also to 'give their assent to the choice of the one' whom the Guardian designates as his successor. (Ed.)

claim to make war, certain rights to impose taxation and all rights to maintain armaments, except for purposes of maintaining internal order within their respective dominions. Such a state will have to include within its orbit an International Executive adequate to enforce supreme and unchallengeable authority on every recalcitrant member of the commonwealth; a World Parliament whose members shall be elected by the people in their respective countries and whose election shall be confirmed by their respective governments; and a Supreme Tribunal whose judgment will have a binding effect even in such cases where the parties concerned did not voluntarily agree to submit their case to its consideration. A world community in which all economic barriers will have been permanently demolished and the interdependence of Capital and Labour definitely recognised; in which the clamour of religious fanaticism and strife will have been forever stilled; in which the flame of racial animosity will have been finally extinguished; in which a single code of international law—the product of the considered judgment of the world's federated representatives—shall have as its sanction the instant and coercive intervention of the combined forces of the federated units; and finally, a world community in which the fury of a capricious and militant nationalism will have been transmuted into an abiding consciousness of world citizenship—such, indeed, appears in its broadest outline, the Order anticipated by Bahá'u'lláh.[9]

In America the administrative work of the Bahá'ís had by 1926 grown so extensive that it was found advisable to bring into being a legal form within which these activities could be more effectively and securely conducted, and a Voluntary Trust was entered into. The terms of this Trust which have been published in *The Bahá'í World* show it to be an effort to apply to certain practical affairs those spiritual principles on which Bahá'u'lláh insisted. It offers itself, therefore, as an example of the Bahá'í philosophy in action in the modern world.

The Declaration of Trust contains seven Articles and its By-Laws twelve, from which the following passages may be quoted as typical.

The latter part of the preamble reads:

> The National Spiritual Assembly in adopting this form of association, union and fellowship, and in selecting for itself the designation of Trustees of the Bahá'ís of the United States and Canada,* does so as the administrative body of a religious community which has had continuous existence and responsibility for over eighteen years. In consequence of these activities the National Spiritual Assembly is called upon to administer such an ever-increasing diversity and volume of affairs and properties for the Bahá'ís of the United States and Canada, that we, its members, now feel it both desirable and necessary to give our collective functions more definite legal form. This action is taken in complete unanimity and with full recognition of the sacred relationship thereby created. We acknowledge on behalf of ourselves and our successors in this Trust the exalted religious standard established by Bahá'u'lláh for Bahá'í administrative bodies in the utterance: 'Be ye Trustees of the Merciful One among men'; and seek the help of God and His guidance in order to fulfil that exhortation.

Towards the close of the Declaration, in Article XI of the By-Laws, occur these striking words:

* Canada formed its own National Spiritual Assembly in 1948. (Ed.)

Among the most outstanding and sacred duties incumbent upon those who have been called upon to initiate, direct and coordinate the affairs of the Cause as members of local or national Spiritual Assemblies are:—

To win by every means in their power the confidence and affection of those whom it is their privilege to serve; to investigate and acquaint themselves with the considered views, the prevailing sentiments and the personal convictions of those whose welfare it is their solemn obligation to promote; to purge their deliberations and the general conduct of their affairs of self-contained aloofness, the suspicion of secrecy, the stifling atmosphere of dictatorial assertiveness and of every word and deed that may savor of partiality, self-centeredness and prejudice; and while retaining the sacred right of final decision in their hands, to invite discussion, ventilate grievances, welcome advice, and foster the sense of inter-dependence and co-partnership, of understanding and mutual confidence between themselves and all other Bahá'ís.[10]

Now, around the world, the activities of the Bahá'ís are carried on in accordance with the ordinances of Bahá'u'lláh set forth and developed by 'Abdu'l-Bahá. A full account of this system and its working, established by the Guardian of the Faith, is given in the later volumes of *Bahá'í World*.*

The avowed purpose of Bahá'í administration, in whatever country it has been established, is to promulgate the knowledge of God, to proclaim the New Gospel of Bahá'u'lláh, and to carry out his desire of peace and unity

* See vol. XIII, Part Two, 'The World Order of Bahá'u'lláh'. The reader is also referred to Esslemont, *Bahá'u'lláh and the New Era*, chap. XV ('Retrospect and Prospect'); and Holley, *Religion for Mankind* (London, rev. ed. 1966), Part II. (Ed.)

among mankind. Its spirit is that of disinterested service. Its motive power is spiritual love. To a place on its councils all men alike are entitled, the brown, the yellow, the red, co-equal with white; 'He is greatest who is nearest to God.' The moral qualifications of all officers are like their official functions exactly and fully defined. The first obligation laid on the members of any group is that of their perfect love and harmony. 'They must be wholly free from estrangement and must manifest in themselves the Unity of God,' said 'Abdu'l-Bahá. His second command was that 'when coming together [they must] turn their faces to the Kingdom on High and ask aid from the Realm of Glory.' The discussion of political matters is wholly forbidden, and business is by order

confined to spiritual matters that pertain to the training of souls, the instruction of children, the relief of the poor, the help of the feeble throughout all classes in the world, kindness to all peoples, the diffusion of the fragrances of God and the exaltation of His Holy Word.[11]

Discipline is strict, and the most complete and whole-hearted unity among the Friends is expected. Every believer is strongly enjoined to

obey with heart and soul [every bidding of the local Assembly] and be submissive unto it, that things may be properly ordered and well arranged. Otherwise [continued 'Abdu'l-Bahá] every person will act independently and after his own judgment, will follow his own desire, and do harm to the Cause.[12]

In neighbourhoods where the Bahá'í Faith is well established the local assemblies have not a little to do, and often carry on much of their work though committees. They seek to promote good feeling among the Friends and to encourage the most earnest co-operation in the Cause. They help the poor, the sick, the disabled, the orphan and the widow, regardless of colour, class or creed. They take the liveliest interest in the material, as well as the spiritual, enlightenment of the young. They maintain correspondence with other Bahá'í centres throughout the world, stimulate the development of Bahá'í publications and magazines, and undertake arrangements for the regular meetings of the Friends, as well as for special gatherings designed to advance the social, intellectual or spiritual well-being of their fellow-citizens. For the sake of efficiency, the procedure in one of these Assemblies is guided by the most modern methods of business; but the spirit which pervades the meeting is one of simplicity and friendliness, and the deliberations of the group resemble nothing so much as those of a family council. Indeed, to the Bahá'í, every community is, like the human race itself, a family, and its interests are best advanced when approached with that knowledge.

Each local Assembly consists of nine elected members, and at the head of all the Assemblies of any particular country is a National Spiritual Assembly which links them all together. This, too, consists of nine members elected, not directly (as are the local assemblies), but indirectly through delegates chosen in each locality for the special purpose. It is the custom to hold elections during the period of the Feast of Riḍván, which celebrates the Declaration of Bahá'u'lláh and runs from April 21st to May 2nd.

Thus a universal system of administration, as well as of economics, of education and of law, with a universal calendar and language, form the five chief instruments of unification which in the name of Bahá'u'lláh were set forth by 'Abdu'l-Bahá in his missionary journey of 1912.

But behind these practical measures there lies a yet more potent unifying force in the general character and influence of the Revelation of Bahá'u'lláh. It induces in all who listen to it a new frame of mind, a new outlook on life, a new realisation of the Unity of God, of his creation, and of the beings whom he has made. It shows that this proposed organisation of many nations into one whole is not an after-thought, a felicitous conception of this latter time. It is, in fact, the normal expression of an ancient and everlasting truth which man has refused to apply or to appreciate. As the human body, though complex and differentiated, is an ordered whole, so is the human race an organic unity. 'One soul in many bodies,' said 'Abdu'l-Bahá. To separate one part from others is to weaken and paralyse. Perfect health and strength exist only when all parts work together in harmony. When all the nations consciously and intelligently group themselves into a single co-ordinated system, then for the first time in human history the race will reach its full strength and vigour. Then it will begin to know itself, to feel its power, to perceive its possibilities, to reach in the life of everyday heights of achievement and felicity of which none of the nations had dreamed in the night of their estrangement.

This unity of mankind is put by Bahá'u'lláh in the setting of a yet greater unity. Man is shown to be by virtue of his material nature no foreigner in his environment nor an alien amid the lower kingdoms of nature. He is the O altitudo of God's creation, yet he is a part of it, and inasmuch as he lives in a body all the beings below him in the scale of life are his lesser brothers and sisters. The whole creative process is one—one in its movement, one in its origin, one in its end. From the Day when the Spirit begins to act upon that primordial substance which fills eternally all space, and moulds it into structures and into yet higher structures till after vast periods of time the elements are evolved and fixed and there appear forms through which the ever-flowing energy of God can manifest itself—from the first premundane stirrings of creation till at last one made in the image of God walks upon the planet and bows his head in worship before his Maker—through this whole process all that happens proceeds from one will, is governed by one law, directed to one purpose and carried through to one last pre-ordained Event. The unity of God is mirrored in all that he does. Man stands at the apex of creation, which exists for him and was undertaken that he might be brought into being. Bahá'u'lláh endorses the ancient quotation from God, 'But for thee I would not have created the spheres.' All men, to whatever race or nation they belong, represent the highest work of the Creator. Each of them, be he white or black, is endowed with all the faculties, and is 'the dawning place of righteousness'.

With such teachings as these Bahá'u'lláh calls on the people of his Dispensation, one and all, to probe the inner meanings of the universe and to enter a new field of consciousness where knowledge of the truth will deliver them from the base delusions that set man against man, nation against nation, race against race.

NOTE

'Abdu'l-Bahá, when establishing the Guardianship, made the Guardian permanent head of the Universal House of Justice and provided, on the principle of primogeniture, for a succession of guardians, who would all occupy this position. However, Shoghi Effendi died without issue in November 1957, some five and a half years before the Bahá'í world community was sufficiently developed, according to his plan, to elect the Universal House of Justice. This institution was, as foreseen by him, elected in 1963 and now perpetuates to the Bahá'í world that divine guidance which is the unique feature of Bahá'u'lláh's Covenant. (David Hofman, *The Renewal of Civilization*, rev. ed., p. 124.)

CHAPTER IX

THE FIRE OF THE KING'S LOVE

Not by divine instruction, not by mind knowledge, nor by the following of a code of law or system of administration is the unification of mankind to be established or inaugurated, but rather by a true abiding love that burns away difference of self-interest, and melts by its flame all hearts into one heart. Each stands for all, and where one is all are.

God in this last and great Day (as the Bahá'ís believe) has fixed upon the earth a Centre towards which all men will turn, a point of attraction that shall draw all men to it and confer upon them for all time a common basis of sympathy and agreement. God has set up his tabernacle among men, has built in their hearts a dwelling-place where his love may enter and abide, and deep in the affections of his children has fixed the firm and everlasting foundation of world-wide concord and unbroken unity. A religion springing from a common aspiration, animated by a common devotion, calling to a common obedience, bestowing upon all a common happiness, shall bind all nations and all lives into one whole by chains of a common awe and a common love.

The labours of all the High-Prophets of the past now have borne fruit. Nothing has been lost. The harvest has come, and to its coming all God's beloved down the ages, the martyrs and the saints, those known to the world and those unknown, all have contributed their share. Daily these are by every believer remembered before God and glorified. The purpose of all the Messengers of God has been to promote among men unity through love.

Know thou [said Bahá'u'lláh in a passage already quoted] that in every age and cycle all laws and ordinances have been changed according to the requirements of the time, except the law of love which, like a fountain, ever flows, and the course of which never suffers change.[1]

When an Indian said to 'Abdu'l-Bahá, 'My aim in life is to transmit so far as in me lies the message of Krishna to the world,' the Master replied, 'The Message of Krishna is the message of Love. All God's prophets have brought the message of Love.'[2]

To a believer, 'Abdu'l-Bahá wrote:

The essence of the teachings of His Holiness Bahá-'u'lláh is Universal Love which comprehends all the virtues of the world of humanity, and is the cause both of eternal life and of the progress of the individuals of the human race.[3]

And again he wrote:

The purpose of the appearance of the Blessed Perfection was the unity and agreement of the people of the world. Therefore, my utmost desire is firstly the accord and union and love of the believers, and after that of all the people of the world.[4]

And in another place:

The first bounty from the True One is love, unity and harmony, and without these all the deeds pass in vain and give no result.[5]

The beginning of this Revelation and its end, is Love. God's love ordained it before the foundation of the world. God's love in his good time has sent it forth in this human realm. God's love has guided, governed and sustained its course. Its three heavenly Light-bearers (its Morning Star, its Sun, its Moon) shed forth in lavish and intense profusion, without stint or limit or cessation, the rays of divine love, scattering the darkness that enveloped the world. They themselves in their own being were love, for God is love and they were of his essence. Their characters and lives were all instinct with love, and so likewise was every command, every teaching they gave. By them love is revealed as the originative and supporting principle of all existence. In *The Hidden Words*, the Voice of God declares: 'Veiled in My immemorial being and in the ancient eternity of My essence, I knew My love for thee; therefore I created thee, have engraved on thee Mine image and revealed to thee My beauty.'[6]

Through all the grades of all that has breath or being, love is the building power, and all is enveloped by the ever-present love of God. Love reflected in the lower kingdoms is the force that gathers primordial and undifferentiated substance into structures and forms, that summons into existence the ancient elements and all their offspring, the fern, the flower, the bird, the beast, and man himself with his transcendent gifts of mind and heart. When in this mortal realm of growth and of decay this attractive power is withdrawn, the combination which it formed is dissolved and disappears. In all the activities of society, love is the force that imparts unity and life, and when in the hearts of men love ceases, the harmony and co-operation, of which it was both the cause and the maintenance, give place to separation and to death.

Love [wrote 'Abdu'l-Bahá in one of his tablets], Love is the principle of God's holy Dispensation, the Manifestation of the All-Merciful, the fountain of spiritual outpourings. Love is heaven's kindly light, the Holy Spirit's eternal breath that vivifies the human soul.

F

Love is the cause of God's Revelation unto man, the vital bond inherent according to divine creation in the essences of things. Love is the one means that ensures true felicity both in this world and in the next. Love is the light that guides in darkness, the living link that unites God with man, that assures the progress of every illumined soul. Love is the supreme law that rules this mighty and heavenly cycle, the sole power that binds together the divine elements of this material world, the supreme magnetic force that directs the movements of the spheres in the celestial realms. Love reveals with unfailing and limitless power the mysteries latent in the universe. Love is the spirit of life within the beautified body of mankind; it establishes true civilisation in this mortal world, and sheds imperishable glory upon every aspiring race and nation . . .[7]

The love of God surrounds every heart, but enters not save as an invited guest. Conscious of his weakness and his misery—of a life so transient, a knowledge so incomplete, a happiness so narrow and unstable—man longs for better things and dreams of a heaven, if one there be. God's love is that heaven, cries Bahá'u'lláh, and summons to it every child of man:

Thy Paradise is My love; thy heavenly home, reunion with Me. Enter therein and tarry not. This is that which hath been destined for thee in Our kingdom above and Our exalted dominion.[8]

'My son, give me thine heart.' To love God is the supreme duty, and the one beatific attainment of each human soul. God waits without. Paradise stands with gates wide open, but only the true lover may enter there. 'Love Me, that I may love thee. If thou lovest Me not, My

love can in no wise reach thee. Know this, O servant . . .
If thou lovest Me, turn away from thyself . . . that thou
mayest die in Me and I may eternally live in thee.'[9] There
is no peace for man nor any glory, save in self-abandoning
love for God; nor though he scour the wide earth and
the highest heaven will he find rest to his soul save in
this love for God. God's love is a stronghold wherein
whoever enters is safe from adversity and distress.

> Bless me with love for Thine Essence [so the votary
> is taught to pray] that being delivered from all regard
> for myself, or for anything but Thee, I may be utterly
> enthralled by Thee, knowing but Thee, seeing nothing
> but Thee, thinking of nothing but Thee.[10]

Love for God is the highest form of wealth man can
gain on earth: it is indeed the only true wealth. 'Whoso
loves Me is the possessor of all things, and he who loves
Me not is indeed of the poor and needy.'[11]

It is the nature of man to love God, would he but perceive and know. God has breathed a breath of his own
spirit into man that man may be his lover. 'My love is in
thee; know it, that thou mayest find Me near unto thee.'[12]
The believer prays, 'Grant me the joy of beholding thy
eternal being, O thou who art more real than myself,
thou who dwellest in my inmost heart.' And if he will but
turn and gaze upon himself he will find God standing
there within him in love, majesty and might. For God's
dwelling-place is not the vaulted sky, and he has no home
on earth save in the heart of his children.

In *The Hidden Words* the voice of God gives poignant
utterance to the lament of an unrequited love. The Great
Lover (who has nothing to gain from his creatures' love,
for all is his already, but has all to give) sorrows over the
infatuation of those Sons of Dust who through their love-

lessness reject their heritage of bliss and bring down upon
themselves a thousand woes. Bahá'u'lláh revealed that the
most important cause of man's evil plight was his lack of
love for God. He set forth four modes of love: God's love
for his own perfections which caused him to create that
these might be known, God's love for man, man's love
for God and man's love for his fellow man. If a fifth be
added, it is, as 'Abdu'l-Bahá said, the love of a man for his
own higher self which causes him to progress. But Bahá-
'u'lláh defined love to be in its essence the turning of man
to God, his severance from all save God, and his desire
for naught save what God desires.

'Abdu'l-Bahá extolled the power created within man by
this love for God.

> By the fire of the Love of God the veil is burnt which
> separates us from the Heavenly Realities, and with clear
> vision we are enabled to struggle onward and upward,
> ever progressing in the paths of virtue and holiness, and
> becoming the means of light to the world.
>
> There is nothing greater or more blessed than the
> love of God! It gives healing to the sick, balm to the
> wounded, joy and consolation to the whole world, and
> through it alone can man attain Life Everlasting. The
> *essence* of all religions is the Love of God, and it is
> the foundation of all the sacred teachings.[13]

There are on earth many semblances and many mock-
eries of the high name of love; but authentic love is rare.
A worldly friend, Bahá'u'lláh taught, in his love for others
is really thinking of himself and his own good; his love is
unreal. '. . . whereas the true Friend hath loved and doth
love you for your own sakes; indeed He hath suffered for
your guidance countless afflictions.'[14]

'Abdu'l-Bahá would warn his hearers against putting

their trust in a love that was not of the truest. He uttered
in his gentle way warnings against a love that was mere
fascination, a love that was based (however subtly) on
self-interest, a love that had its end in antipathy and hate.
A love that has its selfishness or its limits is not enough.
True love in no way seeks its own, nor counts its gifts,
and God in this age demands from his creatures both for
himself and for one another the truth and very reality of
love. 'The true lover of God yearns for tribulation in his
path.' The Báb, Bahá'u'lláh and 'Abdu'l-Bahá with an un-
faltering and a radiant joy, immolated themselves upon
the altar of servitude to God, giving all they had and all
they were up to him utterly. They withheld nothing;
neither their possessions, nor their lives, nor even their
families. They prayed for greater trials yet: 'I never passed
a tree, but Mine heart addressed it saying: "O would that
thou wert cut down in My name, and My body crucified
upon thee, in the path of My Lord!" '[15]

Of the complete Bahá'í it is required that he should love
his neighbour as himself to the extent, if need be, of
sacrificing for him his own comfort and convenience, even
his limb or his life. The brief annals of the Faith record
already how in Muḥammadan countries many a Bahá'í in
perilous times has taken unto himself a brother's fault, or
saved a brother's life, at the expense of his own. Nor is
the Bahá'í to reserve self-sacrifice within the circle of his
comrades or well-wishers. In obedience to God's command, and through the power implanted in him by God,
he must extend his love to all mankind without discrimi-
nation of class or party, race or creed.

Know ye not why We created you all from the same
dust? That no one should exalt himself over the other.
Ponder at all times in your hearts how ye were created.
Since We have created you all from one same substance

it is incumbent on you to be even as one soul, to walk with the same feet, eat with the same mouth and dwell in the same land, that from your inmost being, by your deeds and actions, the signs of oneness and the essence of detachment may be made manifest.[16]

In one of his talks in Paris, 'Abdu'l-Bahá emphasised the boundlessness of true love, and affirmed that now through the gift of the Holy Spirit such love was brought within reach of the sons of men. Love of family, of nation, of race, of party, these and such limited expressions of love were all inadequate.

The great unselfish love for humanity [he said] is bounded by none of these imperfect, semi-selfish bonds; this is the one perfect love, possible to all mankind, and [it] can only be achieved by the power of the Divine Spirit. No worldly power can accomplish this universal love.[17]

No provocation is admitted by God as an excuse for a Bahá'í's lack of love. Loving-kindness is to be a constant impregnable attitude of soul.

The more they oppose thee [wrote 'Abdu'l-Bahá to one whose patience was sorely tried], the more do thou shower upon them justice and equity. The more they show hatred and opposition, the more do thou challenge them with truthfulness, friendship and reconciliation.[18]

In another letter (II, 389) he explained that according to the teachings of Bahá'u'lláh believers must in this present age be the friends of all nations and of all communities. They must not let their eyes dwell upon the violence, the

ill will, the persecution or the hostility that might surround them, but instead should lift their gaze to the realm
of divine glory and look upon these ill-doers as creatures
of God, 'signs of the Lord of signs' who had been brought
into existence by the divine favour and volition, and were
therefore to be regarded, not as strangers or aliens, but as
acquaintances and friends. The believer was not to consider the merits and capabilities of people, but to show
sympathy to strangers as well as to friends, to display
genuine love to others under all conditions, never allow-
ing that love to be overborne by people's hatred, malice,
contentiousness, or spite. If he be made a target for their
arrows, he is to give milk and honey in return; if they
administer poison, he is to bestow sweetmeats; if they
inflict pain, he is to answer with balm.

> Love and faithfulness [he wrote] must so fill the
> heart that men will look on the stranger as a friend . . .
> count enemies as allies, foes as loving comrades, their
> executioner as a giver of life, the denier as a believer,
> and the unbeliever as one of the faithful.[19]

Throughout the teachings this command that the heart
shall be taught and the actions shall express the law of
universal love is set forth repeatedly and insistently, in all
its details and in all its aspects. In that sketch of the good
life, for example, which 'Abdu'l-Bahá gave, and which
has become the viaticum of every Bahá'í, nearly every
injunction is some application of the supreme principle
of love.

To live the life is:

> To be no cause of grief to anyone.
> To be kind to all people and to love them with a pure
> spirit.

Should opposition or injury happen to us, to bear it, to be as kind as ever we can be, and through all, to love the people. Should calamity exist in the greatest degree, to rejoice, for these things are the gifts and favours of God.

To be silent concerning the faults of others, to pray for them, and to help them, through kindness, to correct their faults.

To look always at the good and not at the bad. If a man has ten good qualities and one bad one, look at the ten and forget the one. And if a man has ten bad qualities and one good one, to look at the one and forget the ten.

Never to allow ourselves to speak one unkind word about another, even though that other be our enemy.

To do all of our deeds in kindness.

To cut our hearts from ourselves and from the world.

To be humble.

To be servants of each other, and to know that we are less than anyone else.

To be as one soul in many bodies; for the more we love each other, the nearer we shall be to God; but to know that our love, our unity, our obedience must not be by confession, but of reality.

To act with cautiousness and wisdom.

To be truthful.

To be hospitable.

To be reverent.

To be a cause of healing for every sick one, a comforter for every sorrowful one, a pleasant water for every thirsty one, a heavenly table for every hungry one, a star to every horizon, a light for every lamp, a herald to everyone who yearns for the kingdom of God.

'Abdu'l-Bahá.

What the teachings show, the character and the action of the Messengers themselves show yet more impressively. A perfect love for God and for man is the explanation of their lives, the key to the mystery of their combined achievement. Their laying aside their personal names and assuming spiritual titles signified a complete self-abnega-tion, the sacrifice of all their own ends and purposes for the pursuit of a task undertaken in obedience to God. When Mírzá 'Alí-Muḥammad, the merchant, took the title of the Báb he proclaimed himself the Gate through which the King of Glory was to enter, and dedicated every thought and every moment to making ready in the desert a highway for his Lord.

With a lover's firmness he faced in the Cause of God misunderstanding, misrepresentation and torture, and before he passed the age of thirty met a martyr's death.

Mírzá Ḥusayn 'Alí, at the bidding of the Most High, surrendered rank, wealth and honour, and as Bahá'u'lláh endured half a century of imprisonment, was four times exiled, underwent year by year and day by day countless afflictions, submitting to all with a radiant acquiescence in the will of that Supreme Sovereign whom for love's sake he served.

'Abbás Effendi, born the heir to high distinction and to wide estates, at the age of nine years followed his father into exile, and from that moment to his death at an ad-vanced age made himself as nothing but the servant of the Great Beloved, and counted his title 'Abdu'l-Bahá, 'the Bond-servant of Glory', as his sword and his crown.

The personal appearance of the three as seen in such portraits as are extant bears witness to the same spirit of goodwill and love. The picture of the youthful Báb shows in his face that winning kindliness to which the records testify. In that of Bahá'u'lláh a wonderful sweetness, it is said, is mingled with an expression of authority and massive power. Here is an American's account of his first view of the portrait:

> We looked upon the photograph of Bahá'u'lláh. It is . . . the face of one who had 'found his beloved in the garden' of his heart; in whom a wondrous power was evident, not to oppose but to submit, and submitting to conquer the opposers. There can be no doubt of the source of that wondrous power which sits upon that brow as on a throne of majesty, which rises up, unbidden as a maiden's blush, upon that face with rarest beauty. It is the Blessed Beauty, the Blessed Perfection. It is the face of him in whom no wish nor desire is found save the will of God. It is the Face of God—the lights of all the attributes of God play over it.

In the well-known photographs of 'Abdu'l-Bahá taken in Paris, strength of intellect and will appears in harmony with a great humility and the sadness of a heart that ached in sympathy with a suffering world.

Because a heavenly love was the ruling principle of their activity, the Báb, Bahá'u'lláh and 'Abdu'l-Bahá united to an heroic energy and resolution the gentle beauty and perfections of the saint. Each arose in his place to confront, to defy and to redeem a corrupt, godless and cruel civilisation. In the terrific combat which ensued (a deadly combat in which neither side asked nor gave quarter) the champions of the Most High never lifted a hand in self-defence, never fled from danger, nor showed personal resentment, nor stinted kindness to any, even the meanest and most implacable of their foes. Detesting and denouncing evil, exposing evil-doers and giving battle at any risk to themselves to all who opposed the progress of God's declared will, they yet were compassionate and forbearing, patient, calm, mild.

So radiant was the beauty of the Báb's character that his influence on those about him seemed magical. He would win the hearts even of his jailers, guards, inquisitors. His personal effect upon those about him during his confinement at Chihríq is described by Nabíl, who states that the Governor of the prison found himself powerless to carry out the harsh treatment of the Báb ordered by the Vizír. For

He, too, soon came to feel the fascination of his Prisoner; he, too, forgot, as soon as he came into contact with His spirit, the duty he was expected to perform. At the very outset, the love of the Báb penetrated his heart and claimed his entire being. The Kurds who lived in Chihríq . . . were likewise subjected to the transforming influence of the Báb. Such was the love He had kindled in their hearts that every morning, ere they started for their daily work, they directed their steps towards His prison and, gazing from afar at the castle which contained His beloved self, invoked His name and besought His blessings. They would prostrate themselves on the ground and seek to refresh their souls with remembrance of Him.[20]

Could he have gained access to the head of the Realm, the Sháh, he might have persuaded His Majesty to accept the New Teaching, and have inaugurated an era of reform. His enemies acknowledged and feared the danger. They were ever alert to avoid it. His irregular and hurried execution was especially designed to make such an interview once and for all impossible.

Bahá'u'lláh had the same power of evoking a response to his own outpouring of love.

In the earliest days of the Faith, long before Bahá'u'lláh declared his mission, the poetess Ṭáhirih bore witness to this power: 'The effulgence of the Abhá Beauty hath pierced the veil of night; behold the souls of His lovers dancing, mote-like, in the light that has flashed from His face!'[21]

Professor E. G. Browne, visiting 'Akká in 1890, found him the centre of 'unbounded and almost incredible love and reverence', and on being admitted to his presence described himself as bowing 'before one who is the object of a devotion and love which kings might envy and emperors sigh for in vain!'[22]

The charm and might of that personality is now in the providence of God being withdrawn by time from remembrance, lest men perchance should fall into error, honouring the Superman too much and the Eternal Spirit which shone through him too little. But the servitude to which he inspired his lovers is recorded in history; and it is embodied in its most perfect form in the life, the example, and the name of the Centre of the Covenant.

Only one European is known to have written an account of an interview with the Báb; only one likewise to have recorded an interview with Bahá'u'lláh. But many travellers and pilgrims from the West visited 'Abdu'l-Bahá in his home in Palestine and testified to the warmth and the breadth of his sympathy, his kindness and his charm.

When in his old age, broken in health, he visited the West in an effort to deter men from the war he saw impending, thousands of people in Germany, France, England and America saw him and heard him speak.[23] His genial manner, his quick sympathy, his ever-flowing kindliness, his selfless devotion to the Cause of his Father, were evident to all who had the privilege of meeting him. Physically exhausted, he never declined an opportunity of giving his message. 'Where there is love,' he would say, 'effort is a rest.' There are still many in the Occident as

well as in the Orient who testify to the power of an utterance which touched all hearts and brought to every atten-
tive ear a new knowledge of what is meant by true
goodwill and love.

Of his visit to London, it was written:

> A profound impression remained in the minds and
> memories of all sorts and conditions of men and wo-
> men. The width of Abdul Baha's sympathy proved, in
> every instance, as helpful as his discrimination and
> perspicacity in dealing with difficulties whether subtle
> or obvious. Each person approaching him found him-
> self understood, and was astonished and relieved by
> Abdul Baha's comprehension of religious differences;
> above all, of religious agreements . . . He left behind
> him many, many friends. His love had kindled love.
> His heart had opened to the West and the Western
> heart had closed around this patriarchal presence from
> the East.[24]

> All the people know him and love him—the rich and
> the poor, the young and the old—even the babe leaping
> in its mother's arms. If he hears of any one sick in the
> city—Moslem or Christian, or of any other sect, it
> matters not—he is each day at their bedside, or sends a
> trusty messenger . . . He claims nothing for himself—
> neither comfort, nor honour, nor repose. Three or four
> hours of sleep suffice him; all the remainder of his time
> and all his strength are given to the succour of those
> who suffer, in spirit or in body.[25]

So wrote M. H. Phelps in his *Abbas Effendi*.

Another who knew 'Abdu'l-Bahá (the Governor of
Phoenicia) spoke of him as follows:

> Most of us here have, I think, a clear picture of Sir

'Abdu'l Baha 'Abbas, of his dignified figure walking thoughtfully in our streets, of his courteous and gracious manner, of his kindness, of his love for little children and flowers, of his generosity and care for the poor and suffering. So gentle was he, and so simple that, in his presence, one almost forgot that he was also a great teacher and that his writings and conversations have been a solace and an inspiration to hundreds and thousands of people in the East and in the West . . .[26]

An American meeting 'Abdu'l-Bahá in Thonon recorded his experience as follows:

To look upon so wonderful a human being, to respond utterly to the charm of his presence—this brought me continual happiness . . . Patriarchal, majestic, strong, yet infinitely kind, he appeared like some just king that very moment descended from his throne to mingle with a devoted people . . . He laughed heartily from time to time—indeed, the idea of asceticism or useless misery of any kind cannot attach itself to this fully-developed personality. The divine element in him does not feed at the expense of the human element, but appears rather to vitalize and enrich the human element by its own abundance, as if he had attained his spiritual development by fulfilling his social relations with the utmost ardour.[27]

When in November, 1921, 'Abdu'l-Bahá passed away, one of the tributes paid to him included these words:

The eyes that had always looked out with loving-kindness upon humanity, whether friends or foes, were now closed. The hands that had ever been stretched forth to give alms to the poor and needy, the halt and the maimed, the blind, the orphan and the widow, had now finished their labour. The feet that, with untiring zeal, had gone upon the ceaseless errands of the Lord of Compassion were now at rest. The lips that had so eloquently championed the cause of the suffering sons of men, were now hushed in silence. The heart that had so powerfully throbbed with wondrous love for the children of God was now stilled. His glorious spirit had passed from the life of earth, from the persecutions of the enemies of righteousness, from the storm and stress of well nigh eighty years of indefatigable toil for the good of others.[28]

These quotations, culled almost at random, suggest something of the impression made on those Westerners who met and knew him. The classic expression of the inspiring power which he could impart to one prepared to receive it is from the pen of one of the writers cited above.

. . . as the party rose I saw among them a stately old man, robed in a cream-coloured gown, his white hair and beard shining in the sun. He displayed a beauty of stature, an inevitable harmony of attitude and dress I had never seen nor thought of in men. Without having ever visualized the Master, I knew that this was he. My whole body underwent a shock. My heart leaped, my knees weakened, a thrill of acute, receptive feeling flowed from head to foot. I seemed to have turned into some most sensitive sense-organ, as if eyes and ears were not enough for this sublime impression. In every part of me I stood aware of Abdul Baha's presence. From sheer happiness I wanted to cry—it seemed the most suitable form of self-expression at my command. While my own personality was flowing away, even while I exhibited a state of complete humility, a new being, not my own, assumed its place. A glory, as it were, from the summits of human nature poured into me, and I was conscious of a most intense impulse to admire. In Abdul Baha I felt the awful presence of Baha'o'llah, and, as my thoughts returned to activity, I realized that I had thus drawn as near as man now may to pure spirit and pure being. This wonderful experience came to me beyond my own volition. I had entered the Master's presence and become the servant of a higher will for its own purpose. Even my memory of that temporary change of being bears strange authority over me. I *know* what men can become; and that single overcharged moment, shining out from the dark mountain-mass of all past time, reflects like a mirror I can turn upon all circumstances to consider their worth by an intelligence purer than my own.[29]

Such is the love that God has breathed upon the dead heart of the world. Such is the love which is to reawaken the souls of men to the consciousness of heavenly things and to quicken their spirits to a higher life. Already it has shown its efficacy in great and in little. It has lent a new charm to social converse. It has broadened vision, it has broken barriers, it has sweetened life, it has taught a daring and a fortitude to which there seem no bounds. In the early days of the Faith it used to be said that one could not take tea with the Bahá'ís without wishing to join their society. The Persian Muslims ascribed the attractive power of the Friends to the use of philtres and magic charms whereby they infected their neighbours with their own madness. The eagerness, the ardour, the rapture which filled the hearts and souls of those early Bábís, is indeed (even to those who can only read now the record of it) a wonder, an inspiration and a challenge. With what longing, what boundless enthusiasm they rejoiced to spend themselves in devotion to their Lord. No effort was too difficult to make, no danger too serious to court, if only thereby they thought they could serve his Cause. Those possessions which they, like other men, held dear—property, reputation, comfort, home, child, wife and life itself—these they were ready to abandon for their dear Lord's sake, and counted it the greater blessing if by making some complete outstanding abnegation they might the better show the full measure of their love and give the greater glory to the Báb and to his God.

The Báb (himself a living flame from which all others in those earliest days caught their fire, and which in its intensity and power none else could rival or approach)— the Báb in the perfection and the passion of his spiritual love was the original and great exemplar of them all.

Once when in a vision some of the Báb's friends expressed to him fear of his personal safety, he answered:

> Fear not . . . I am come into this world to bear witness to the glory of sacrifice. You are aware of the intensity of My longing; you realise the degree of My renunciation. Nay, beseech the Lord your God to hasten the hour of My martyrdom and to accept My sacrifice. Rejoice, for both I and Quddús will be slain on the altar of our devotion to the King of Glory. The blood which we are destined to shed in His path will water and revive the garden of our immortal felicity. The drops of this consecrated blood will be the seed out of which will arise the mighty Tree of God, the Tree that will gather beneath its all-embracing shadow the peoples and kindreds of the earth.[30]

That sacred adage which Nabíl applies to the martyr Quddús would seem to apply with scarce less accuracy to many of his fellow-Bábís:

Whoso seeketh Me, shall find Me.
Whoso findeth Me, shall be drawn towards Me.
Whoso draweth nigh unto Me, shall love Me.
Whoso loveth Me, him shall I also love.
He who is beloved of Me, him shall I slay.
He who is slain by Me, I Myself shall be his ransom.[31]

If another quotation from that heroic age be needed to show the spirit of the Bábís at that time, it may be the outcry of the young Ḥujjat when, in the persecution of Zanján, he had just seen his dear wife and their infant killed.

> . . . though filled with grief [he] refused to yield to idle sorrow. 'The day whereon I found Thy beloved One, O my God,' he cried, 'and recognised in Him the Manifestation of Thy eternal Spirit, I foresaw the woes that I should suffer for Thee. Great as have been until now my sorrows, they can never compare with the agonies that I would willingly suffer in Thy name. How can this miserable life of mine, the loss of my wife and of my child, and the sacrifice of the band of my kindred and companions, compare with the blessings which the recognition of Thy Manifestation has bestowed on me! Would that a myriad lives were mine, would that I possessed the riches of the whole earth and its glory, that I might resign them all freely and joyously in Thy path.'[32]

Baffled in their efforts to check this influence, the mullahs, through a persistent persecution to which already reference has been made, sought to destroy good with evil, and to kill love with hate. The new faith was proscribed and its votaries subjected to a violent and unrelenting persecution. The Bábís, and afterwards the Bahá'ís, were insulted, driven from their homes, impoverished, beaten, exiled, paraded under torture through the streets, beheaded, torn limb from limb, or massacred indiscriminately by scores and hundreds. Knife and bludgeon, boiling water and slow fire: these and such as these were the weapons of the priesthood against the objects of their wrath. Few of the faithful shrank from the torture; few hesitated; many went to their death singing in exultation the love song of the martyrs, and bore their sufferings with benedictions on their lips. Thousands thus have given their lives for the Bahá'í cause.

As of old, so now, the blood of the martyrs is the seed of the Church. The love which God had kindled in the world lived on unquenched and undimmed. It spread far and wide, east and west, traversing continents, leaping seas, consuming all barriers, checked by no bounds. Its influence has been felt up to the present time by but a small section of the human race. Yet already under the banner of Bahá'u'lláh men of many tongues and diverse loyalties stand united by a bond more strong than that of common gain or common blood. The divine love reflected in their hearts has burned away prejudice and misunderstanding, and made them one. To such men as these the wide earth is one kingdom and one home, where all men think, feel and act as brothers beneath the aegis of a Father-King.

This love now pouring down from God in fullest measure upon the awakening consciousness of mankind is the power that will regenerate human nature, and will create in deed and in fact a new heaven and a new earth.

CONCLUSION

Such is Bahá'u'lláh's teaching on the original and essential unity of the human race, on the unity of its religions, on the unity of its divinely guided development.

Such too is the story of Bahá'u'lláh's endeavour to bring to men tidings of the millennium and to inculcate in them the ideal of universal harmony and the practice of universal peace.

Is there in all this no message to a world sinking ever deeper into political and economic distress, struggling on from broken hope to broken hope, saddened by disillusion, sickened by disappointment, haunted by increasing fears, and seeking to forget its miseries in headlong extravagance and passionate excess?

Since the first edition of this work was published the progress and the consolidation of the Bahá'í Cause has been the most signal and hopeful achievement in the spiritual history of the times.

The Faith has shown itself proof against those disintegrating forces which have corroded the fabric of human society, have shaken or destroyed its institutions and have brought about the fall of its proud and mighty civilisation. While a disillusioned and visionless world was drifting from misery to misery, from one uncontrollable crisis to another, it has spread East and West till it has reached more than eighty* countries; it has preserved the integrity and exaltation of its teachings; has co-ordinated its expanding activities; has developed its administrative Order and has animated its followers with an enthusiasm which

* See p. 15, footnote.

carries them continually forward to new ventures, to new triumphs.

It is fitting, therefore, that this edition (more especially since the author has now identified himself with the Bahá'í Faith) should close on a yet stronger note of hope and assurance than before. To all who can see the spiritual situation of the world as a whole, it is manifest that humanity will never build a new civilisation, nor escape from the wreckage of the old, except by adopting in their fullness the plans and counsels of Bahá'u'lláh.

Will not the religious leaders and thinkers of the West examine thoroughly and without prejudice, the high claims of Bahá'u'lláh? And will they not, discerning the true Source and spiritual nature of this supreme Epoch of Transition, lead their churches into the heavenly Jerusalem, so that all Christendom may arise for the regeneration of mankind?

BIBLIOGRAPHY

'ABDU'L-BAHÁ. *Abdul Baha in London*. Addresses, & Notes of Conversations. Chicago: Bahai Publishing Society, 1921.

—— *Paris Talks*. Addresses given by 'Abdu'l-Bahá in Paris in 1911–1912. First published 1912. 11th British ed. London: Bahá'í Publishing Trust, 1969; repr. 1971. Published in the United States under the title *The Wisdom of 'Abdu'l-Bahá*. Wilmette, Illinois: Baha'i Publishing Trust.

—— *The Promulgation of Universal Peace*. Discourses by Abdul Baha Abbas During His Visit to the United States in 1912. Vol. I, Chicago: Executive Board of Bahai Temple Unity, 1922. Vol. II, Chicago: Baha'i Publishing Committee, 1925.

—— *Some Answered Questions*. Collected and Translated from the Persian of 'Abdu'l-Bahá by Laura Clifford Barney. First published 1908. London: Bahá'í Publishing Trust, 1961. Published in the United States by Bahá'í Publishing Trust, Wilmette, Illinois.

—— *Tablets of Abdul-Baha Abbas*. (Referred to as *Epistles* by Mr. Townshend.) Chicago: Bahai Publishing Society, Vol. I, 1909; Vol. II, 1915; Vol. III, 1916.

ABU'L-FAḌL, MÍRZÁ (Mirza-Abul-Fazl). *The Baháï Proofs*, Hujaju'l Beháyyeh. Chicago: The Grier Press, 2nd ed. 1914.

Bahá'í World, The. An International Record. Vol. II (1926–1928), Vol. IV (1930–1932), Vol. IX (1940–1944). New York and Wilmette, Illinois: Bahá'í Publishing Committee, 1928, 1933 and 1945, respectively.

Vol. XIII, 1954–1963. Haifa, Israel: The Universal House of Justice, 1970.

BAHÁ'U'LLÁH. *Epistle to the Son of the Wolf.* Trans. by Shoghi Effendi. Wilmette, Illinois: Bahá'í Publishing Committee, 1941.

—— *Gleanings from the Writings of Bahá'u'lláh.* Trans. by Shoghi Effendi. New York: Bahá'í Publishing Committee, 1935. Wilmette, Illinois: Bahá'í Publishing Trust, rev. ed. 1952, repr. 1969. London: Bahá'í Publishing Trust, 1949.

—— *The Hidden Words.* Trans. by Shoghi Effendi. London: Bahá'í Publishing Trust, rev. ed. 1949, repr. 1966. Wilmette, Illinois: Bahá'í Publishing Trust, 1954, with Introduction by George Townshend.

—— *The Kitáb-i-Íqán. The Book of Certitude.* Trans. by Shoghi Effendi. New York: Bahá'í Publishing Committee, 1931. Wilmette, Illinois: Bahá'í Publishing Trust, 2nd ed. 1950, 3rd repr. 1960. London: Bahá'í Publishing Trust, 2nd ed. 1961.

—— *The Proclamation of Bahá'u'lláh* to the kings and leaders of the world. Haifa: Bahá'í World Centre, 1967.

—— *The Seven Valleys and The Four Valleys by Bahá'u'lláh.* Trans. by Ali-Kuli Khan (Nabílu'd-Dawlih), assisted by Marzieh Gail. Wilmette, Illinois: Bahá'í Publishing Trust, rev. ed. 1948, repr. 1957.

BLOMFIELD, LADY (Sitárih Khánum). *The Chosen Highway.* London: Bahá'í Publishing Trust, 1940. Reprinted Wilmette, Illinois: Bahá'í Publishing Trust, 1967.

BROWNE, E. G. (ed.), *A Traveller's Narrative written to illustrate the Episode of the Báb.* Vol. I, Persian Text. Vol. II, English Translation and Notes. Cambridge University Press, 1891.

CHEYNE, T. K., *The Reconciliation of Races and Religions.* London: Adam & Charles Black, 1914.

ESSLEMONT, J. E. *Bahá'u'lláh and the New Era*. An Introduction to the Bahá'í Faith. First published London: George Allen & Unwin Ltd., 1923. Wilmette, Illinois: Bahá'í Publishing Trust, 3rd rev. ed. 1970.

NABÍL-I-A'ZAM (Muḥammad-i-Zarandí). *The Dawn-Breakers*. Nabíl's Narrative of the Early Days of the Bahá'í Revelation. Wilmette, Illinois: Bahá'í Publishing Trust, 1932, repr. 1953. London: Bahá'í Publishing Trust, 1953.

SHOGHI EFFENDI. *Bahá'í Administration*. First published 1928. Wilmette, Illinois: Bahá'í Publishing Trust, 1968.

—— *God Passes By*. Wilmette, Illinois: Bahá'í Publishing Trust, 1944. 5th repr. 1965.

—— *The Promised Day Is Come*. First published 1941. Repr. Wilmette, Illinois: Bahá'í Publishing Trust, 1961.

—— *The World Order of Bahá'u'lláh*. First published 1938. Rev. 1955. 2nd impr. Wilmette, Illinois: Bahá'í Publishing Trust, 1965.

—— and SITARIH KHANUM (Lady Blomfield). *The Passing of 'Abdu'l-Baha*. Stuttgart: 1922.

ZAEHNER, R. C., *Hinduism*, Oxford University Press, 1962.

NOTES

Names of authors and titles of books are usually abbreviated in these notes; full details are given in the bibliography. Page numbers are given for American and British editions of the same book when the reference could not otherwise be identified. For some quotations later sources and translations are used than those available to the author, but where older translations are quoted, they were sometimes edited by the author. Titles and quotations are reproduced in their original form.

INTRODUCTION

1. *Abdul Baha in London*, p. 2. He wrote in Persian, to which this translation was added.

2. *ibid.*, p. 6.

3. Blomfield, p. 168.

4. Cheyne, pp. 159 and 161.

5. *ibid.*, pp. 8–9.

6. *ibid.*, p. 5.

7. *ibid.*, p. 209.

8. *ibid.*, cited pp. 213–14.

9. Paris, 1865; 3rd ed. 1933.

10. Browne, *Traveller's Narrative*, vol. II, pp. 202–3.

11. Curzon, G. N., *Persia and the Persian Question* (London, 1892), vol. I, pp. 503 and 501.

12. *ibid.*, p. 503.

13. Browne, *Traveller's Narrative*, vol. II, xxxviii–xxxix.

14. *ibid.*, xxxix–xl.

15. *Christian Commonwealth*, 22 January 1913; cited *Bahá'í World*, vol. IX, p. 568.

16. Cited *Bahá'í World*, vol. IX, p. 570.

17. *ibid.*

18. Younghusband, Sir Francis, *The Gleam* (London, 1923), pp. 210–11.

19. Cited *Bahá'í World*, vol. XIII, p. 818.

20. *ibid.*, p. 804.

21. *ibid.*, p. 806.

22. 'Abdu'l-Bahá, *Promulgation*, vol. I, p. 4.

Chapter II. The Self-Manifestation of God

1. Bahá'u'lláh, *Book of Certitude*, p. 64 (Brit.), p. 99 (U.S.).
2. *ibid.*, pp. 64–5 (Brit.), pp. 99–100 (U.S.).
3. These are not necessarily the exact words of the Báb, but their substance is correct. See Shoghi Effendi, *World Order*, pp. 109 and 113 for similar statements by Bahá'u'lláh.
4. 'Abdu'l-Bahá, *Some Answered Questions*, ch. XLII.
5. Bahá'u'lláh, *Gleanings*, xxii.
6. Bahá'u'lláh, *Book of Certitude*, p. 14 (Brit.), p. 20 (U.S.).
7. *Abdul Baha in London*, p. 33.
8. 'Abdu'l-Bahá, *Epistles*, vol. I, p. 138.
9. Cited Bahá'u'lláh, *Book of Certitude*, p. 98 (Brit.), pp. 152–3 (U.S.). See also Qur'án, ii. 285 and liv.50.
10. Bahá'u'lláh, *Book of Certitude*, p. 113 (Brit.), p. 176 (U.S.).
11. *ibid.*, p. 114 (Brit.), p. 178 (U.S.).
12. Qur'án, xv. 21.
13. From 'The Valley of True Poverty and Absolute Nothingness'.
14. 'Abdu'l-Bahá, *Some Answered Questions*, ch. XLI.

Chapter III. The Succession of the High-Prophets

1. Davids, Mrs. C. A. F. R., *Buddhism* (London, 1912), pp. 33–4.
2. Bahá'u'lláh, *Book of Certitude*, p. 14 (Brit.), p. 21 (U.S.).
3. Nabíl, pp. 1–2 (Brit.), p. 2 (U.S.).
4. Qur'án, xxxix. 68.
5. Nabíl, p. 32 (Brit.), pp. 41–2 (U.S.).
6. *ibid.*, p. 93 (Brit.), p. 134 (U.S.).
7. *ibid.*, p. 229 (Brit.), pp. 315–16 (U.S.).
8. Bahá'u'lláh, *Book of Certitude*, p. 63 (Brit.), p. 97 (U.S.).
9. *ibid.*, p. 84 (Brit.), p. 130 (U.S.).
10. *ibid.*, pp. 69–70 and 72 (Brit.), pp. 107–8 and 111 (U.S.).
11. 'Abdu'l-Bahá, *Some Answered Questions*, ch. XLII.
12. Bahá'u'lláh, *Book of Certitude*, pp. 3–4 (Brit.), p. 4 (U.S.).
13. *ibid.*, p. 5 (Brit.), p. 6 (U.S.).
14. *ibid.*, p. 3 (Brit.), pp. 3–4 (U.S.).
15. *ibid.*, pp. 9–11 (Brit.), pp. 13–17 (U.S.).

CHAPTER IV. THE MISSION OF THE LORD CHRIST

1. Esslemont, ch. XI; an alternate translation.

CHAPTER V. THE VIGIL OF THE DAY OF DAYS

1. The verses quoted are from Vaughan's 'Primitive Holiness' (see *The Works of Henry Vaughan*, Oxford, 1957, p. 349), and Dryden's 'A Song for St. Cecilia's Day 1687'.

2. In *De Vita Caesarum, Divus Vespasianus* IV.

3. Esslemont, ch. I.

4. *Shaykh Aḥmad* (A.H. 1157–1242, *circa* A.D. 1743–1826) began his mission in 1793 and was joined by Siyyid Kázim in 1815–16. See Nabíl.

5. Nabíl, p. 4 (Brit.), pp. 4–5 (U.S.).

6. Browne, *Traveller's Narrative*, vol. II, p. 235. See also Nabíl, p. 1, n. 2 (U.S.).

7. Nabíl, p. 19 (Brit.), p. 25 (U.S.).

8. *ibid.*, pp. 31–2 (Brit.), pp. 41–2 (U.S.).

CHAPTER VI. THE GATE OF THE DAWN

1. Nabíl, p. 108 (Brit.), p. 154 (U.S.).

2. Cited Shoghi Effendi, *World Order*, p. 101.

3. Nabíl, p. 53 (Brit.), p. 77 (U.S.).

4. *ibid.*, p. 54 (Brit.), pp. 79–80 (U.S.).

5. *ibid.*, p. 219 (Brit.), p. 303 (U.S.).

6. Cited Shoghi Effendi, *World Order*, p. 126.

7. Nabíl, pp. 63–5 (Brit.), pp. 92–4 (U.S.).

8. *ibid.*, p. 285 (Brit.), p. 396 (U.S.).

9. Browne, *Traveller's Narrative*, vol. II, p. 309.

10. Nabíl, p. 455 (Brit.), p. 622 (U.S.).

11. Cited Shoghi Effendi, *God Passes By*, p. 65.

CHAPTER VII. THE ENTRANCE OF THE KING OF GLORY

1. Browne, E. G., *A Year Amongst the Persians* (Cambridge, 1926), pp. 111–12.

2. Muslim traditions cited by Bahá'u'lláh in *Son of the Wolf*, pp. 178–9.

3. Cited Shoghi Effendi, *God Passes By*, p. 184.

4. Nabíl, pp. 5–6 (Brit.), p. 8 (U.S.).

5. Bahá'u'lláh, *Hidden Words* (Persian), no. 23.

6. Bahá'u'lláh, *Son of the Wolf*, p. 56.

7. *ibid.*, p. 59.

8. *ibid.*, p. 108.

9. Bahá'u'lláh, *Proclamation*, pp. 59–60, and Browne, *Traveller's Narrative*, vol. II, p. 147.

10. Bahá'u'lláh, *Hidden Words* (Arabic), no. 51.

11. Bahá'u'lláh, *Proclamation*, p. 60.

12. Bahá'u'lláh, *Son of the Wolf*, pp. 94–5.

13. *ibid.*, p. 107.

14. Browne, *Traveller's Narrative*, vol. II, p. 147.

15. Bahá'u'lláh, *Son of the Wolf*, p. 53.

16. Browne, *Traveller's Narrative*, vol. II, pp. 91–2.

17. Bahá'u'lláh, *Hidden Words* (Arabic), preamble.

18. *Bahá'í World*, vol. II, p. 59. See also *Bahá'í World Faith* (Wilmette, Illinois, 1943), pp. 140–1.

19. Cited Shoghi Effendi, *World Order*, p. 135.

20. Cited Shoghi Effendi, *Promised Day*, p. 62.

21. Bahá'u'lláh, *Gleanings*, lvi.

CHAPTER VIII. THE LIGHT OF THE KING'S LAW

1. Bahá'u'lláh, 'Words of Wisdom'; see ch. VII, n. 18.

2. Bahá'u'lláh, *Hidden Words* (Persian), no. 76.

3. Browne, *Traveller's Narrative*, vol. II, pp. 113–15.

4. Bahá'u'lláh, *Hidden Words* (Persian), no. 82; and (Arabic), no. 68.

5. *ibid.* (Persian), no. 64.

6. *ibid.* (Arabic), no. 2.

7. Bahá'u'lláh, 'Words of Wisdom'; see ch. VII, n. 18.

8. Browne, *Traveller's Narrative*, vol. II, xl.

9. Shoghi Effendi, *World Order*, pp. 40–1. From 'The Goal of a New World Order', November 28th, 1931.

10. See *Bahá'í World*, vol. XIII, pp. 547 and 554.

11. Cited Shoghi Effendi, *Bahá'í Administration*, p. 22.

12. *ibid.*, p. 21.

CHAPTER IX. THE FIRE OF THE KING'S LOVE

1. See ch. IV, n. 1.

2. 'Abdu'l-Bahá, *Paris Talks*, p. 35 (Brit., 1971), p. 30 (U.S.).

3. 'Abdu'l-Bahá, *Epistles*, vol. III, p. 544.

4. *ibid.*, vol. II, p. 125.

5. *ibid.*, p. 183.

6. Bahá'u'lláh, *Hidden Words* (Arabic), no. 3.

7. *Bahá'í World*, vol. II, p. 50.

8. Bahá'u'lláh, *Hidden Words* (Arabic), no. 6.

9. *ibid.*, nos. 5 and 7.

10. The author's paraphrase of lines in Bahá'u'lláh, *Seven Valleys*, 'The Valley of Knowledge'.

11. Bahá'u'lláh, 'Words of Wisdom'; see ch. VII, n. 18.

12. Bahá'u'lláh, *Hidden Words* (Arabic), no. 10.

13. 'Abdu'l-Bahá, *Paris Talks*, p. 82 (Brit., 1971), p. 74 (U.S.).

14. Bahá'u'lláh, *Hidden Words* (Persian), no. 52.

15. Cited Shoghi Effendi, *Promised Day*, p. 42.

16. Bahá'u'lláh, *Hidden Words* (Arabic), no. 68.

17. 'Abdu'l-Bahá, *Paris Talks*, p. 37 (Brit., 1971), p. 32 (U.S.).

18. 'Abdu'l-Bahá, *Epistles*, vol. III, pp. 557–8.

19. *ibid.*, vol. I, p. 125.

20. Nabíl, pp. 218–19 (Brit.), p. 302 (U.S.).

21. *ibid.*, p. 205 (Brit.), p. 286 (U.S.).

22. Browne, *Traveller's Narrative*, vol. II, xvii and xl.

23. 'Abdu'l-Bahá also visited Switzerland, Austria, Hungary and Canada.

24. *Abdul Baha in London*, xiii–xiv.

25. Phelps, M. H., *Life and Teachings of Abbas Effendi* (New York, 2nd ed. 1912), pp. 6 and 10.

26. Shoghi Effendi, *The Passing*, p. 20. Also Balyuzi, H. M., *'Abdu'l-Bahá* (London, 1971), p. 481.

27. Holley, Horace, *Bahaism: The Modern Social Religion* (London, 1913), Appendix I. Also Holley, *Religion for Mankind* (London, rev. ed. 1966), pp. 233 and 235.

28. Shoghi Effendi, *The Passing*, p. 9. (The words quoted are the authors'.) Also Balyuzi, *'Abdu'l-Bahá*, p. 464.

29. Same as n. 27 above.

30. Nabíl, p. 98 (Brit.), pp. 140–1 (U.S.).

31. *ibid.*, pp. 50–1 (Brit.), p. 72 (U.S.).

32. *ibid.*, p. 419 (Brit.), p. 572 (U.S.).